THE
VOICE
THAT
CALLS YOU
HOME

ANDREA RAYNOR

THE
VOICE
THAT
CALLS YOU
HOME

INSPIRATION FOR LIFE'S JOURNEYS

ATRIA BOOKS
New York London Toronto Sydney

ATRIA BOOKS
A Division of Simon & Schuster, Inc.
1230 Avenue of the Americas
New York, NY 10020

First Atria Books hardcover edition November 2009

ATRIA BOOKS and colophon are trademarks of Simon & Schuster, Inc.

For information about special discounts for bulk purchases, please contact Simon
& Schuster Special Sales at 1-866-506-1949 or business@simonandschuster.com.

The Simon & Schuster Speakers Bureau can bring authors to your live event.
For more information or to book an event contact the Simon & Schuster Speakers
Bureau at 1-866-248-3049 or visit our website at www.simonspeakers.com.

Designed by Davina Mock-Maniscalco

Manufactured in the United States of America

10   9   8   7   6   5   4   3   2   1

Library of Congress Cataloging-in-Publication Data

Raynor, Andrea.
    The voice that calls you home : inspiration for life's journeys /
Andrea Raynor.—1st Atria Books hardcover ed.
        p. cm.
    1. Spirituality. 2. Consolation. 3. Death—Religious aspects.
4. Terminally ill—Religious life. I. Title.

BL624.R3925 2009
204'.42—dc22
                                                    2009036193

ISBN 978-1-4165-9611-0
ISBN 978-1-4391-0070-7 (ebook)

For my children
Cat and Alex

Come, come, whoever you are,
Wanderer, worshipper, lover of leaving—
    it doesn't matter,
Ours is not a caravan of despair.
Come, even if you have broken your vows a
    hundred times
Come, come again, come.

—Rumi

CONTENTS

INTRODUCTION

M OST OF US HAVE experienced some sort of trauma in our lives. Perhaps it is the loss of a child, a spouse, or a parent; or perhaps it is the trauma of living in these uncertain times—times when, as we found out, death can come on the bluest of days to people sitting at their desks or dozing on an airplane. Maybe you, like me, like so many of us, are looking for some hope, some inspiration, some toehold on life so that we are better prepared to cope with the challenges that are sure to come.

This yearning to make sense of the things that befall us can be the catalyst for spiritual growth. And yet it requires courage. If we are willing to move beyond simplistic rationalizations of why bad things happen, we may find ourselves in unfamiliar territory. What if everything *doesn't* happen for a reason? What if it just happens? When we surrender our idea of the Divine as a sort of Grand Puppeteer or Superhero, we are left with a God who can seem utterly unwilling or unable to protect us. How are we to live with that?

Simply speaking, when we most need reassurance, God can feel inaccessible and remote. This is especially true if we have thought of God as our insurance policy against bad things happening—our just-in-case genie that we keep stashed away for emergencies. When times are good, many of us don't think much about the Divine; but when faced with true hardship, accompanied by what feels like God's silent acquiescence, deep down, we mourn. We mourn the assurance that we are loved and protected by Someone or Something Greater than ourselves.

What if we could live each moment knowing that we are not forgotten, but rather are loved and cherished, precious and fully known, regardless of circumstance? What would this mean for our lives? What would we see? How would we live? What would we hear in the dark night of despair if we listened, not for the response of a magic genie but for the rumblings of a voice deep within—the echoed song of the One who is home to our Spirit? It might sound something like "Do not be afraid. Do not be afraid. I am with you."

How do we hear this voice? Perhaps God speaks to us in the only voice God has—that of creation. God speaks through the people we encounter, through those who face devastating hardships without losing hope, through those who suffer heartache and yet somehow still know joy, and through those who survive spiritually though the foundations of their faith have been rocked. God speaks through the beauty of nature, through the perfection of a snowflake, through the light coming in—just so—from a window. If we open our hearts and minds to the messages that come to us, we will discover that life is inherently meaningful despite the hardships we bear, and that we are not alone on the journey. For the weary and the wounded, this is rest for the soul.

As a chaplain, I have searched for ways to offer comfort in times of suffering. When I was diagnosed with cancer myself, I was suddenly on the receiving end of comfort. What I found in my work and in my life is that sound theology and eloquent words can only do so much, usually soothing but the surface of the wounded heart. Words can be a balm, yes, especially if they are the right words, but the only thing that truly heals is presence—being present to the pain of the sufferer and allowing that person to tell his or her story without plugging the holes that grief has left like ragged buckshot. Hopefully all of us have had the experience at one time or another of being heard and understood and can recall the healing this inspired.

Part of the secret to surviving hardship, then, is being willing to share our stories and to be present to one another. By doing so, we will discover the muscular resiliency of the heart. We will experience the restorative cycle of the breath—the exhalation of our own stories, the inhalation of the stories of others. Give and take, ebb and flow, crying and comfort. It is the respiration and resuscitation of the soul. It is the way of compassion. Rumi, the thirteenth-century Persian poet, described it this way:

Your hand opens and closes and opens and closes.
If it were always a fist or always stretched open,

you would be paralyzed.
Your deepest presence
is in every small contracting and expanding,
the two as beautifully balanced and coordinated
as birdwings.*

THERE IS A Buddhist tale that beautifully illustrates this. It is about a woman named Kisagotami, who has suffered the loss of her infant son. Racked with grief, Kisagotami cannot accept his death. And so she carries the baby's body to the Buddha, begging him to bring her son back to life. The Buddha listens to her anguish, then sends her away with this instruction: She must go back into her village, and if she can return with a single mustard seed from a household that has not known death, he will restore her son to her. As one might expect, Kisagotami returns to the Buddha empty-handed— but something has happened to her in the process, something has been changed and healed in her. Maybe she has come to accept that hers is a universal fate, that all have experienced or will experience the loss of a loved one—but somehow, I do not believe this is the whole story.

After working with many families over the years, I have learned that it is seldom comforting to remind them that others, too, have suffered. Others have lost mothers and fathers, sisters and brothers, children and spouses. And it is never comforting to compare one person's pain with someone else's. Acknowledging the suffering of others may help to normalize our

* Coleman Barks, "Birdwings," in *A Year with Rumi: Daily Readings* (San Francisco: Harper San Francisco, 2006), p. 17.

experience, it may ease the feeling of being isolated in grief, but it will not ultimately free us from pain. Reason and intellect seldom soothe the heart. Wise Buddha knew this . . . and so he gently sent Kisagotami on a path toward self-discovery, a path that she could walk or crawl at her own pace, a path free from judgment—the only path that could lead her to acceptance and healing.

So what was it that ultimately consoled Kisagotami in her search for the mustard seed? What happened as she went door to door, telling her story and having to hear the stories of others? At first, one can imagine that she pounded on each door with the raw anguish of a mother's grief, pleading, begging, hoping for a different answer than the one that was sure to come. "Please, please, you've got to help me! Please tell me that you have not been touched by death. What's that? You have? But you don't understand—my son has died, my little boy, and I have to find a way to bring him back to life."

Each time she entered a new home, Kisagotami was forced to tell her story and to bear the disappointment of leaving without the mustard seed—and, therefore, without hope that her child could be brought back to life. In each home, she told her tale and she listened to the stories of the ones who lived there. Each family who welcomed her must surely have recognized the desperation born out of love for her child; each could feel the pain of this young mother and could empathize with her refusal to accept her child's death. No doors were slammed in her face, no one refused her entrance; no one mocked her for her attempt to find the mustard seed. Perhaps the compassion of others started to soften the sharp edges of her grief. Perhaps

the stories that she collected going from home to home began
to be interwoven with her own veil of sorrow. What thread was
her loss, what the old woman's, what the young man's? What
color was her broken heart, now braided into a rainbow cord of
stories? Only Kisagotami knows for sure what began to shift in
her, and what brought her back to the feet of the Buddha free
from bitterness and despair. But clearly, when she stood before
him again, she did so with a new sense of purpose and a heart
filled with compassion.

The secret of the mustard seed is one that we all must discover for ourselves. It doesn't matter what condition we are in
when we begin. We can be bitter, we can be raging mad at
God, insane with grief, unrealistic, self-absorbed, anguished,
or zombielike. The only thing that matters is our willingness
to undertake the journey—to knock on one more door, to
hear one more story—and to let the stories begin to work their
way into our hearts and into our lives. Perhaps we will discover
that we are not alone. Perhaps we will be soothed by the compassion of others who have suffered, and we will experience
ever more deeply the profound comfort of being heard and
held by those who know. Along the way, we may also have the
privilege of offering comfort to someone else, of extending a
small cup of kindness to one in need. In any case, the journey
is at once individual and communal. It is a path which winds
through the darkest forest but moves us ever closer toward the
light—a light that promises to break in the clearing ahead.

How we view our experiences can dramatically change our
perception of God's presence as well as our sense of well-being.
What if we could revisit the events that shaped our lives, espe-

cially those times of despair, and see emerging through the dim and hazy images the comfort that was always there, the Presence that never abandoned us. Living with an awareness of the Holy means opening our eyes to beauty, to the grace that pervades everyday interactions, and to the expectation that something extraordinary could happen—is happening—at every turn. God's absence is only our illusion.

All of us will someday face adversity; all will wrestle with a traumatic event. We may not be able to prevent these or even to anticipate them, but we can always choose the way in which we will respond. We can surrender to despair or we can embark on a journey of spiritual exploration. The path may not be easy, but it will be illuminated. Torches have been lit by those who have gone before us, and they promise to guide us out of the darkness toward the clearing ahead. We need only to keep moving, gathering strength, gathering light, following our innate spiritual compass, for it always points toward home.

If we trust in the journey, we will begin to see that life is inherently blessed. It is infused with meaning—some of which we might grasp and some of which will remain a mystery. We, too, are part of that mystery. We have been set on our course like stars since the beginning of time—propelled into motion—hurtling now through space, traveling at our own velocities, burning at our own speeds, and dying in our own times. How will we live? We can live with our heads down, our eyes closed, and our hands in our pockets, or we can open ourselves to catch the blessings that fall, softly and silently, like moonlight and sunlight, like mist before dawn.

* * *

WE ARE PART of the Great Constellation. The stardust in our bones draws us to the heavens like a magnet, like a homing signal for the soul. Nothing can change this. Not hardship, not death—not even a lack of faith. This is simply how we are made. If we tune in to the frequency, the Voice that calls us, chances are that our spirits will become lighter, stronger, more courageous, more compassionate—and life itself will seem an incredible adventure.

HOLY GROUND

As I STEPPED OUT of the elevator on the fifth floor of Lawrence Hospital, the halls seemed strangely quiet. It was 8:00 PM—long past the time that I would normally be seeing patients for hospice. Then again, this was an unusual case.

I had received a call from one of our nurses informing me of a young, male patient at the hospital. He was twenty-eight years old and was actively dying from a rare type of lung cancer. If he lived through the night, the plan was to try to bring him home to die. The chances of this happening did not look good. Although there was little that could be done for him medically, besides keeping him comfortable, the nurse thought that his family might benefit from some spiritual support.

I wasn't sure what I would find when I arrived. I had been told that the man had a wife and a three-year-old daughter in addition to his mother, who rarely left his side. I walked down the corridor to the nurses' station, mindful of the hushed atmosphere. For some reason, it felt more like a convent than a hospital. The quiet lent an air of gravity; it seemed to press itself upon my chest. I steadied myself, trying not to worry about what I might say, who I might find, in the room of the young man and the mother I was about to meet. What could one ever say to a mother who was losing her child? *Just be present,* I reminded myself. *Be present.*

With a nod, the nurse on duty indicated the direction of the patient's room. Without saying a word, her eyes told me that this man was dying, and dying soon. No, more than that—they conveyed wave upon wave of sadness. They searched my face for a moment as if to say, "Can't you do something? Can't you extract something from that deaf-mute God of yours?" It was clear that this was going to be a difficult night—for the patient and his family first and foremost, and for the staff, who would be standing by like those unable to stop a tidal wave.

"His mother is with him," the nurse said softly. "His wife went home a couple hours ago. She couldn't bear it. Plus, she has their daughter to worry about. But his mom . . . his mom is amazing."

When I entered the room, it was like stepping into a small sanctuary—not that it looked like one by any stretch of the imagination, but it felt like one. The lights were dimmed, and from a radio came the soft sound of an organ playing hymns and spirituals. The woman at the patient's bedside had the presence of a holy woman, a guardian angel, a shaman—Mary, Shiva, Eve. In a flash, she was every mother whose heart is breaking and she was this particular woman losing this particular son. Her presence was so powerful, it seemed she could rip the universe in two with her bare hands if it meant giving her child life.

Our eyes met. She, an African American woman with an intense, steady gaze and a forgiving face, and I, a young, white mother and minister. She was welcoming and yet protective; and it was clear that she was prepared to do whatever it might take to guard her son, ensuring that his last hours would be filled with peace and love. I was immediately aware of the reality that I would have little to offer this woman beyond my deep respect and reverence. Truth leads to humility, and humility to wisdom. I didn't know much, but I was wise enough to recognize that my presence was not a gift to her—it was a privilege granted to me by this woman.

"I only want him to hear pleasant things now," she said softly but with authority.

I nodded. Moving closer to the bed, I had the urge to take off my shoes, for I felt that I was standing on holy ground. We stood facing each other on either side of the bed. I was grateful for the cool, metal bed rails, which gave me something to hold on to, something with which to steady myself. Then I took him in. He was quite possibly one of the most beautiful men I have ever seen. Though diminished by illness, his features were stunning—the smooth forehead and strong, dark brows, the graceful curve of his cheekbones, the strength of his sculpted nose. His mouth was open, revealing the perfect arc of straight, white teeth beneath full lips. I exhaled—devastated, awed.

"He is a beautiful man, your son."

"Yes, he is," the woman answered. "Yes, he is. More than

you could ever know. He is a wonderful father and husband, and he is my son."

I tore my eyes away from his face and caught a glimpse of some pictures on the windowsill beyond his mother's shoulder. There, smiling back at me, was his daughter, with the flashing eyes of a toddler and her father's bone structure; there was his wife, smiling, too, still blissfully unaware of the random way in which illness chooses its victims.

"How's your daughter-in-law?" I ask.

"Not good. I sent her home. She's got the baby to take care of now. But I am his mother. He had a good life—it wasn't a long life, but it was a good one. I brought him into the world, and I will rock him home."

We stood in silence at his bed. His breath came in labored, uneven wheezes; the air smelled like death. I was aware of the gurgle in his chest, the "death rattle," as it is commonly known. His head was turned toward his mother, and his eyes were slightly open. She had his hand in hers, but in spirit she had his whole body, cradling it like a child's. The Pietà incarnated. I offered to read a few psalms, I offered a prayer—but mostly I offered another mother's broken heart. Then I left the hospital, knowing that I would never see either of them again.

I got in my car and drove a block or two before pulling into a parking spot in front of a natural foods store that I frequented. I'm not sure why I did that other than being vaguely aware of the need to collect myself before I went home. As I went inside to buy a bottle of water, I saw Robyn, the owner of the store, who was starting to close up for the night. She was about ten years older than I, a naturally beautiful woman with

long dark hair, smooth olive skin, and two teenage children of
her own. She took one look at me and asked if I was okay. I
started to tell her about my visit to the hospital . . . and then I
began to weep. The tears would not stop as I tried to describe
to her the beauty of the man and his mother, and the sacred
space she had created out of a sterile hospital room. Robyn put
her arms around me, and we stood like that for a moment in
the empty store. Then she took my hand and led me to another aisle, saying, "Here. Come here. Take this—it'll help." I
looked at the small brown bottle that she pressed into my
palm. Homeopathic Rescue Remedy.

"It won't fix anything, but it helps. Take the water, too.
And don't even think of handing me that money. Do you need
anything else?"

"No, Robyn. But thanks, thanks so much."

When I walked into my house, it was quiet—not the quiet
of the hospital, with its weighty and ominous silence, but the
quiet of children sleeping, the quiet of every night we take for
granted, the quiet that embraces us like an old friend, descend-
ing without so much as a whisper of thanks.

I took off my shoes and walked up the stairs to my children's bedrooms. For the longest time, I stood at my son's bed.
As I rested my hands on the warm, curved wood of his little
crib, I couldn't help but think about the stainless steel rails of
the young man's hospital bed. I could picture that mother gazing upon her son as I was gazing upon mine. My son's breath
came softly and steadily; it smelled like sweetgrass and milk.
His fingers instinctively curled around mine as I stroked his
palm.

There is nothing I can do to protect my son, I thought. *There is no prayer I can pray, no promise I can make, no deal I can strike with God or the devil to ensure his safe passage through this life.*

Then I felt myself falling through space, tumbling through my childhood conceptions about God, about protection, about the unspoken agreement I'd always felt I had with the Big Guy. If you tried to be good, tried to pray and to be faithful, wasn't God supposed to shield you? Wasn't God supposed to hold up his end of the bargain and secretly cut you a break? Intellectually, I knew this was primitive and childish thinking, but emotionally, I was grasping for straws. *If that mother, that powerful, faithful, godly mother at the hospital could not protect her son,* I thought, *then I am doomed.* What would I give to protect my children? Only everything. Only everything. But now, the only thing I could give was my terrified acknowledgment that I was powerless, that God was powerless, and that prayer seemed a ridiculous exercise in wishful thinking.

Standing there, I remembered an article I had read in the *New York Post.* The cover had caught my eye with one of its famous screaming headlines. It read: KISS YOUR ASTEROID GOOD-BYE! Intrigued, I bought a paper and browsed the articles on what was thought to be an asteroid heading straight for earth. Dear old planet earth, floating there like a sitting duck in a puddle of space, unable to get out of its own way, much less the way of a rogue asteroid. Scientists warned that it was heading our way, and if it hit us, well, that would be it for the planet.

Along with the scientific data, there was a small, humorous

blurb about a Florida insurance company that was selling "anti-asteroid coverage." For a one-time charge of $19.95, a person could buy lifetime coverage against damage from an asteroid. This coverage included damage to one's liver from excessive drinking as a result of worrying about asteroids, hair loss (for the same reason), and the chiropractic care needed from craning one's neck. The only problem was, if an asteroid really hit, who was going to collect from whom?

It was a silly article; but as I stood before my son's crib, the irrational lengths to which we are prepared to go to buy safety for ourselves and our loved ones seemed understandable. I would buy it. I bought the idea as a child that God would keep me safe, safe in the dark, safe as I babysat; that God would intervene if a stranger reached out to grab me. I believed that God safeguarded the good and those who talked to him as often as possible, as if to remind him, "Hey, I'm here."

All I could do was stand there in the darkness of my son's little room and let the tears fall. I sent my love through the night air, through the particles that make up atmosphere and oxygen, solid space and bodies with their living cells. I sent my broken heart to the mother standing before her son's bed just two miles from me. I held her hand, with her son's hand, as I held my own son's.

Don't let them go, I thought/prayed. They were standing in the path of the comet, but they were without fear. Maybe that's all we can do. Pray for the strength to bear what comes in life. Pray, even if we stop believing that there is Someone who hears. Pray so that we do not die inside. Pray because it keeps the heart beating, it synchronizes us with nature, with the ebb and flow of the tide, with the moon and the stars, and with all the rest of creation, which (like us) has no control over what is set in motion by random events and by what we will never understand. If this woman could believe in God, even as she watched her son die, that was enough for me. Who was I to dishonor her with my doubt?

Somewhere, light-years away, an asteroid would drift out of earth's range. Maybe it was headed for another planet, maybe it would collide with a star, maybe it would lose momentum and become but another grain of sand in that ocean of universe. In the meantime, the earth would continue to spin, and her people would continue to bear and lose their young, to do the best they can, and to whisper a prayer every now and then, to anyone who might hear: "Hold us, Lord, and don't let go."

2

YANKEE SWAP

ONE OF THE MORE horrific experiences I have had as a hospice chaplain came not with a patient, not with a family, not at the bedside, but rather at a holiday staff party. For years, the memory of it made me cringe and shudder. I felt ashamed, embarrassed—outed as a charlatan and poseur. Only when I retold the story recently to my best friend was I really able to let it go and to laugh about it . . . to see it in a different light and to forgive myself.

I had been working with hospice for about eight months. During this time, questions of meaning, of suffering, of the randomness of illness, of God's presence or absence, of faith and prayer and what gives comfort, all of these were being raised by my patients and by myself. Their soul-searching prompted my own. Their pain caused me to wring my hands in anguish, questioning the very foundations upon which I had built my faith. The worst I could do, I decided, would be to offer easy answers; the best I could do was to simply offer myself.

As the months passed, I became more comfortable with the open-endedness of our discussions, and more adept at slipping in and out of the homes of our hospice families. I didn't take it personally when someone would hesitate before accepting a visit from me. After all, what could I do? And what did I represent? Unlike the nurse, whose visit meant relief from physical suffering, or the reassurance that a loved one was doing okay, or the delivery of needed medications, the chaplain signified (for many) "the end," last rites, making peace before and with death.

The social workers and I would humorously jockey for position at the bottom of the hospice team totem pole. The heart of their work is similar to mine, of course—offering support to the dying and to their families—but there is also a practical component to social services, making their entrée less threatening. The social workers are part of the intake process, meeting patients and families as they sign on to the program and establishing the crucial face-to-face rapport that helps to open doors for them later. When I call, I have the sense that many are picturing the shadow of the grim reaper with his sharp, curved sickle standing just over the right shoulder of my disembodied voice. The thinking is that, when the priest comes to call, death cannot be far off.

I understood this, and I learned to navigate around and through it. My fellow team members came up with ingenious ways of helping me get through the door for that first visit— delivering diapers and urinals, rubber gloves and bed pads, picking up or dropping off papers, or simply tagging along. Once I was inside, the response was almost always positive. "Well, you're not so scary," people would often say. Or "You're a lot prettier than my priest." Or "I just didn't know what to expect." What had been a challenge for me in the beginning of my ministry—being young and female and not exactly what one would call a traditional-looking pastor—became an asset. I was not the guy in the collar, the guy many were (fairly or not) afraid of. I was simply someone to talk to, someone who would pray with them, or help them contemplate the afterlife, or simply look through family photos, as if searching for some clue to the mystery of who they were. I looked like their daughters or granddaughters, their friends or their sisters. They intuited that I would not judge them if they questioned their faith or if they had no idea of what they believed in. They could be "bad Protestants," "lapsed Catholics," "nonpracticing Jews," agnostics, or atheists. They could be afraid, raging mad at God, or fully looking forward to the life to come. In short, they did not have to pretend to be at peace; they did not have to prove they were good people. They could just be.

This is not to say that I always said or did the right thing. There were plenty of times I put my foot in my mouth, especially in those first months. Times I would get back into my car after a visit and pound my head on the steering wheel, wishing I could take something back, do something better, offer a little more in the way of reassurance or theological reasoning or counseling. These times of failure, I knew, were working me, softening me, honing me into a better chaplain, and a more helpful presence. Most times, however, I would return to my car filled with profound images of courage and love, aware of the privilege of having been allowed into yet another stranger's home.

Learning how to be a good chaplain to my patients was not the only challenge. I also had to win over some of my teammates—and the difficulty of this took me by surprise. We were, for the most part, an organization of women. Over the eleven years that I was associated with this particular hospice, I knew only two men who were full-time employees—one nurse and one social worker. Being naïve, I assumed that the women would be natural allies for me, but this wasn't always the case. Perhaps it was because I was relatively young when I started my work there, still nursing my son and tending to my toddler daughter. To some, this may have made me appear less professional. Or maybe it was that most of the staff happened to be Catholic and were used to a more traditional type of pastor, or that the previous chaplain sometimes wore a collar, which I never did. Maybe it was my long hair, my relaxed attitude, my natural tendency toward the funky side that made them secretly skeptical of me. Whatever the case, I often felt like I was pushing against an immovable force when it came to gaining the trust and respect of my colleagues—but I refused to be anyone other than myself. As my best friend once said when we were in divinity school: "It's hard being me . . . but the older I get, the more I realize that I don't really have a choice!" For some reason, it always sent us into spasms of laughter when we thought of that.

When the annual holiday party rolled around, I was still feeling like the new kid at school. Everyone seemed to know what to bring, what to wear, what to expect. I scurried around asking questions. Did you bring your spouse? Was it casual? Should I bring my kids? In the midst of this, I was told that one of the traditions at the party was to participate in what is known as a "Yankee Swap." The phrase still sends chills down my spine.

Yankee Swap is basically a game of calculated gift stealing. Perhaps that's a little harsh. Most people think it's fun. It goes like this: Everyone brings a wrapped gift within an agreed upon price limit. Next, each person draws a number. The first person opens a gift—then waits like a sitting duck for the next thirty people to decide if they want to keep the one *they* have just opened or take someone else's. It is a true case of "the last shall be first," because the person with the last number has her pick of *all* of the gifts. He or (in our case, most likely) *she* will have the final triumphant say over which gift is most desirable, most coveted. As luck would have it, I happened to draw the highest number, giving me that last say. Immediately, I felt the mixed-baggedness of this simple twist of fate. Naturally, I had that secretly delighted feeling of having won the prize, of having landed the golden egg. And yet . . . I also sensed the creeping dread of responsibility, and the horror of my coming moment in the spotlight.

As the game began, we sat in a casual circle in the lovely living room of one of the nurses. There were peals of laughter as some gifts were opened. These were obvious "re-gifts" from the year or two before, inside jokes that stitched the team together in camaraderie and years of service. There were a few oohs and aahs when the occasional pretty scarf or ingenious use of fifteen dollars was revealed—and more laughter when these were snatched away by the next person.

About midway through the game, a couple of items became favorites, changing hands almost every time someone took a turn. One of these was a bowl-size ceramic cup, which included either a packet of dried soup mix or some tea, I can't remember which. It bounced around the room like a beach ball, causing mock outrage from each person from whom it was stolen. I watched as the pile of unopened gifts dwindled, surveying the booty which would be mine for the picking.

One of the last people to go was one of our per diem nurses, Fran. I didn't know her well because, soon after I began, she had been diagnosed with breast cancer. Fran worked through most of her treatment, though I cannot for the life of me figure out how. She had a large family, with children ranging from middle school to college, and she was determined to keep things going for them as long as possible. Fran was brave, funny, down-to-earth—a good nurse and a strong mother. She refused to allow her cancer to take center stage— although it was beginning to nudge her toward the sidelines. I would often see her talking quietly to one of the other nurses in the office, but I felt shy about trying to offer my support. I was new. I was this strange Protestant chaplain. Fran was beloved. She had support. She had friends. She was a religious Catholic from a strong Polish family. She was kind to me; but now, looking back, I think she sensed her time was limited, and letting new people into her intimate circle just took too much energy. Besides, it might remind her that she was dying.

When it came Fran's turn for the Yankee Swap, she exchanged what she had opened for the ceramic cup. That's when I began to sweat. I had decided a few turns ago that I would go for the cup. Not only was it the most practical of the gifts but it seemed to get the most laughs whenever someone swiped it. Now what would I do? Could I take it from Fran? Dear Fran? Fran who had breast cancer, who everyone knew wasn't doing well? If I took it from her, would everyone think me callous, shallow, a hypocrite? Would it confirm their suspicions about me? But, if I *didn't* take it, everyone (including Fran) would know it was because she was sick. I started to get a sick feeling myself. Should I treat Fran just like, well, Fran, and take it, or should I treat her like *sick* Fran and leave it? Would she think this patronizing, highlighting her illness, or would she be just as glad to catch a little break?

Before I could figure it out, all eyes were upon me. It was my turn, the final round. *Just go for the leopard scarf,* I told myself. *That's the way out. No, better not, too racy . . . that will confirm that I am a lunatic. Sex book? Funny, ironic even, but probably worse.* People were smiling, curious, egging me on. What would I pick? *Treat Fran like Fran,* I thought. Barely aware of what I was doing, I found myself rising from my chair, rising and walking toward Fran . . . and the cup. "I'll take the cup," I said with a smile. Instead of laughter, there was silence. Stunned, horrified, condemning silence. I'd messed up.

Suddenly, I was four years old again. It was Christmas Eve, and we were on our way to my aunt Zella's house in Kentucky. We were packed tightly into our family car, six of us wedged together by heavy winter coats and bulky wrapped presents, by dishes of scalloped potatoes and green beans and Tupperware containers protecting apple pies still hot from my mother's oven. My father was pointing toward a flashing light in the sky—a light we strained to see—suggesting we better not stay too long, lest Santa find us out of bed. My mother was in profile as she turned to remind us about the surprise for my aunt. I could see her pretty nose, which sloped slightly and perfectly upward, her blond hair pulled back in a stylish ponytail. I thought that she was the most beautiful and powerful person on the planet. My mom—a tiny Grace Kelly in her five-foot frame, smarter than anyone else, a better cook, tireless and selfless and fair.

"Remember," she was saying. "The present for Aunt Zella is a secret. She has always wanted the camels that go with her Nativity set—the one Aunt Anna Bell brought from Costa Rica. She doesn't know that we've got a pair for her. This is going to be a very special surprise."

We all nodded excitedly. Two of my aunts, Aunt Anna Bell and Aunt Ginny, were missionaries in Costa Rica. They didn't visit often, but when they did, they would bring interesting things like coffee-bean necklaces and embroidered napkins and leather footstools with pretty engraved patterns. One year, they had given my mother and grandmother hand-carved Nativity sets. Zella had admired them so much that they sent another one to her. But ours had included beautiful wooden camels, carved in smooth detail, which added to the strangeness and mystery of the scene. When Christmas rolled around, Zella would joke about wanting to spirit them away to her own Nativity. Now, we had her camels in hand—and they were going to be a big hit.

Throughout the evening, the suspense was growing. We children were naturally wild with anticipation—not just for this particular evening but for the morning to come—for Christmas and presents and the melee of flying wrapping paper and piles of boxes, and for all the sounds and smells that meant life was bursting with happiness. We were one night away. The only thing between Christmas morning and us was this one night—and two camels.

As presents began to be passed out and opened, Zella would occasionally ask one of the children, "Do you know what's in this box for me?" We would shake our heads and giggle, eyes practically popping out of our heads with the image of those camels pressed against our temples, hands clasped against our mouths to hold the secret in. Either someone had tantalized her with the idea that she was receiving something special or she already knew, or she was just trying to engage us children in the excitement. Whatever the case, I was fully onboard. Every time she would taunt one of us to tell her what the box contained, we would hold our sides and roll on the floor like cartoon kittens.

Finally, for what seemed to be the millionth time, she turned to me, looking me full in the face. Her blue eyes were wide and twinkling, and her soft Kentucky accent fell like butter on my ears. "Come on now, Andie. Surely *you'll* tell me what's in this box!" For a split second, I was caught off guard. Was she truly asking me to tell? My four-year-old mind was in a tangled ethical dilemma. I *did* know what was in that box, and my aunt was asking me to tell her. Wasn't she? *Wasn't she?* Everyone was looking at me, smiling. My aunt was coaxing with her wide eyes and her honeyed voice, "Come on now, you can tell me." The pressure was building. I could take it no longer. "CAMELS! THERE ARE CAMELS IN THAT BOX!" I shouted, gleeful, triumphant, bursting with benevolence. I looked around, smiling broadly into . . . silence. Dead silence. Embarrassed, disappointed, I-could-kill-you silence. I had ruined the surprise. I had ruined Christmas.

Riding home, I pressed my forehead to the cool window of the backseat. I tried to hide the large, hot tears that ran down my cheeks. How could I have blurted out the secret? I was miserable, confused, separate from the rest of the family. I stole a glance at the back of my mother's elegant neck and winced. She was being stoic in the face of my disgrace. How could I explain that I had fallen for the trap? That it really wasn't my fault? At that moment, way down below in the belly of my spirit, something slammed shut. I would have to learn how to be careful now. I would learn to keep quiet. Things weren't always the way they appeared. I'd been set up.

When the cup passed into my hand from Fran's, I knew immediately that I'd made a mistake. There was the same silence. The same embarrassed conclusion to what had been, moments before, the merriment of gift giving. *Oh shit. Oh no. Not again.* "I'm sorry, Fran. You keep it," I tried to say.

"No, no. Don't be silly," she said, shaking her head and smiling. Was it my imagination, or did her shoulders sag just a little when she handed it to me—an imperceptible sigh escaping from one who really hadn't gotten a break with this illness?

I felt a chill in the room. Awkwardly, I tucked the cup under my chair in an attempt to hide it, and couldn't wait for the party to be over.

Fran died just a few months after our holiday party. For the next eight years, I could not bring myself to use that cup. I put it toward the back of my cupboard, I moved it around, I even thought of giving it away. But for some reason, I left it there, beating against the cabinet door like a telltale heart. I wanted to hit myself over the head with it every time I saw it sitting impassively there on the shelf. I replayed the scene, trying to remind myself why I had decided to take the cup in the first place, trying to justify it. Then finally one day, I pulled it out and plopped a tea bag in it. *Hello, Fran,* I thought. *Please forgive me. Would you mind if I used your cup?*

Now when I open my cabinet, I see the cup and simply think of Fran. Because of it, I have kept her close to me, she whom I barely knew. At first, that cup living in my cupboard made me wince. It was my daily peck on the liver, my penance for a deed I could not take back. But slowly, as I forgave myself, I could feel Fran's forgiveness. And I began to let the albatross slide from my neck.

I know it's silly that a game of Yankee Swap would torture me so, but it had come to symbolize a lack of compassion and wisdom on my part. It became a reminder to listen more closely, to pay more attention, to be more present to the suffering of others. The cup also inspired me to remember Fran every day, to hold her close in my heart and to pray for her children. Through the years, I would occasionally see one of her sons, who worked at a local department store. His face, wide and sweet and welcoming, would invoke images of that open cup—a cup into which I had poured many prayers, and many petitions for wisdom and forgiveness. Perhaps, one day, I will hand him the now faded and well-worn prize and tell him that it had belonged to his mother.

When I was diagnosed with cancer, I took out that cup and made myself a giant cup of tea. I sipped it slowly and put myself in Fran's chair the night of the party. How would I have wanted to be treated? Like everyone else? Like me without cancer? I realized that was impossible—*that* me was no more. In my mind, I watched myself slowly approaching the Fran-me. *Come on, give me a break,* I heard myself thinking. *I've got cancer and I'm probably going to die. Let me keep the damn cup.* That was the real Yankee Swap—putting myself in her place. What I regretted taught me, and what I learned was not simple. In fact, I'm learning still.

Some things are not our fault. Blurting out "Camels" as a child is not the same as taking a sick woman's cup, even though the overall effect invoked a similar shame in me and shocked horror in others. Perhaps the adults who were present on that ill-fated Christmas Eve should have done a swap with me. Nobody tucked me close and told me it was okay; nobody tried to fill the embarrassed silence that magnified my mistake. Perhaps this is because it wasn't as big a deal (at least to them) as I remember. But in my mind, I was left with the misery of my terrible big mouth and the feeling that I had ruined everything.

It can be an uncomfortable proposition, swapping places, till all the numbers are called, till we have to give it all away, till we acknowledge our selfishness, till we learn to let go, till we feel what the other feels. There are going to be cups in our cabinets, talismans of our momentary blunders—but there will be camels, too, who have traveled great distances, just waiting to be set free.

3

CALABRESE SUN

THE OLD MAN TOOK his leave quietly. It had been a long night, a long few months, and a longer journey. He left after everyone had a chance to say their good-byes, to wish him well, and to tell him how much he meant to them. *It's time,* he thought. *Better to leave before I'm ready than to stay too long.*

He looked around the bedroom. The winter sun knocked against his window, filling the room with colorless light. It was not the sun of Calabria, with its burnt yellow glow, but it was warm through the glass. *Too early to think of spring,* he mused, *but seductive enough to get on my way.* He paused to listen to the voices coming from the kitchen. Shutting his eyes, he smiled and breathed a deep sigh of contentment. *The music of the home,* he thought. *What can compare?* It was almost enough to make him change his mind about going. Hesitating, he thought again about the sun this time of year in Calabria. He thought about the blue-green of the sea, and the tomatoes as big as your fist, about the men sipping espresso as they argued over local politics, and about the rocky hills he had climbed as a child. *I shouldn't keep them waiting,* he thought, turning toward the window once more, a beam of sunlight igniting the gold in his eyes.

A few minutes later, his wife appeared at the door. She knew that he was gone before her toes crossed the threshold, before her ears heard or her eyes were able to see. His absence passed through her body like light or sound, invisible yet measurable. She moved quietly to the side of the bed and placed her hand on his head. "Nunzie," she whispered. "Nunzie." But he was still. She put her cheek against his pillow and allowed the wordless river of grief to carry her. She surrendered to it, she welcomed it. She wanted to be washed away in it—washed away to the place where her husband had gone. "Nunzie," she breathed.

By the time I arrived, the family was beginning to gather. I had not met any of them before this moment, before the nurse had called asking for me to come and offer a prayer. I slipped quietly into the home and introduced myself to the patient's daughter, son, and wife. After a few minutes, I asked if I could enter the man's room. "Of course, of course" was the warm reply. There was a reverent silence in the room as people stood around his bed. Strangely enough, it felt not unlike the hushed awe of viewing a newborn for the first time. Nunzio's wife of seventy years, Mrs. C, sat by his side, gazing at his face—a face so familiar that every feature, every expression must have been engraved upon her heart. Even this, this alabaster moment frozen by a last breath, possessed an intimacy that made me look away out of respect.

I stood on the other side of the bed, across from Mrs. C, and placed my hand on his head. "He looks very peaceful," I said softly to no one in particular.

"Yes," said a voice at my side. It was his daughter. "He was just talking to us this morning—he even ate a little breakfast and asked my brother to shave him. His nurse was here. After she examined him, we stepped into the kitchen for a moment and when my mom went back into the room, he was gone. He was gone."

I nodded. Then the family began to speak, expressing gratitude that Nunzio had died in the morning rather than in the middle of the night, that he was comfortable and peaceful, and that the nurse had happened to be present. They shared little things about his life—things he was proud of, like his award for being a fifty-year member of the union. They recounted his near fatal accident as a young man when a brick fell on him from six stories up, joking that it was only his hard Calabrian head that saved him! Then, quietly, they told of his recent health struggles, his hospital stays, and his final journey home.

More family arrived. I offered, as I always do, to say a prayer. We squeezed into the small bedroom, and I was aware of a momentary awkwardness. They were Italian Catholics, and obviously, I was not. I smiled, apologizing to the family for being a Protestant. "There is only one God," the daughter said with a warm smile. And so I prayed. I offered thanks for his life, I prayed for God to receive Nunzio's soul into the company of the saints of light; I prayed for comfort for the family and strength for the days ahead. Finally I invited them to join me in the Lord's Prayer. We stood there quietly for a few moments, then the nurse said that she was going to ask everyone to step out of the room. She explained that she needed to get Nunzio ready before the people from the funeral home arrived to pick him up.

Catching the nurse's eye, I asked her, "Are you really going to ask the family to leave?"

"That's correct." She smiled. "I usually do so that I can prepare the body."

"What do you need to do?" I pressed, thinking there might be a wound or a dressing that would be upsetting for the family to see.

"Well, I'm just going to tidy him up a little so that he can leave here clean and with dignity."

"That's great," I nodded, "but why don't we ask Mrs. C if she wants to stay in the room with us? After all, she has been caring for his body for seventy years."

"Good idea," the nurse replied. "Beautiful."

When she turned to ask Nunzio's wife if she wanted to stay while we prepared her husband's body, I shut my eyes and let out a small sigh. It still surprises me that even the best professionals forget sometimes. Even the kindest and most compassionate are tempted to take over, forgetting how important it is to give the family choices, especially at the time of death.

As I had suspected, Mrs. C did not hesitate in her response—she wanted to remain present. It was a desire she never would have asserted, in part because of her generation's respect for medical authority and in part, perhaps, because her primary language was Italian. Had we not asked her, she would have been denied an intimate and beautiful good-bye— and we would have missed an incredible expression of love.

When all of the family but Mrs. C had left the room, the nurse asked the home health aide to bring a clean, warm washcloth. When the aide returned with it, she started to hand it to the nurse. Instinctively, my hand went out to intercept it— then I asked Mrs. C if she would like to wash her husband's face. She nodded silently. What we witnessed next took my breath away.

Mrs. C took the washcloth and, without saying a word, she gently began to wash her husband. Her touch was graceful, and achingly tender. She started with one side of his face, smoothing his brow, caressing his ear, following the curve of his nose and his nostrils. Then she kissed his forehead and kissed it again. She proceeded with the same silent dance on the other side of his face, wiping his brow, his forehead, his ear, his nose. She caressed his mouth, moistening his lips with the wet cloth, bathing it with her eyes and her memories. She then cleansed his neck and collarbone. It was so intensely intimate, this anointing, this saying good-bye to the face and the man whom she had loved for seventy years—it was so holy— that tears welled in my eyes and threatened to pour down my cheeks. I exhaled slowly, knowing that there would be time later to acknowledge how this woman had touched me. But out of respect for her, and the deep awareness that this was her moment, I steadied myself and surrendered to the mystery of what was happening there.

She kissed him once more, then asked the nurse to give her some lotion. She smoothed it on his face, caressing his features with her hand, lingering over his nose, his chin, his lips. When she was finished, she nodded to us, indicating it was time to move on to his arms. The momentum was undeniable now. The hush in the room, the light through the window, the power of this woman's devotion, surrounded and held us in place. *Watch,* whispered a voice from somewhere within me. *Watch and bear witness.*

We uncovered his right arm, and she began to bathe it—the forearm and wrist, the fingers, and all the crevices in between. Without looking up, she held out her palm and said with the quiet authority of a surgeon requesting an instrument, "Lotion." The nurse squeezed some lotion into Mrs. C's open hand, and she smoothed it over her husband's arm, his elbow and hand. She worked it around his fingers, rubbing each one slowly, rhythmically. She repeated the ritual on his left arm, and then started on his legs and feet, his ankles and toes.

We (professionals) stood by mesmerized. We were awed by the power of all that clearly remained between this man and this woman, and the beautiful way in which this was revealed in her anointing of him. I thought of how long women had been preparing the bodies of the dead. Thought of the women who went to prepare Jesus' body after he died, only to find him gone. And, I thought of whose face I might anoint with such tenderness and love. And who would gaze upon my dead face in that way.

Who do we want with us at the end of the day, when "the

shadows lengthen and the light grows dim"? Who will assume the Authority of the Intimate in caring for our dead bodies? For my dead body? Will there be someone to wash us and claim us, and to remind the professionals that they are but guests in our homes and in our lives? Mrs. C's face and actions stunned me—not because I had an unrealistic picture of an idyllic marriage but because it was clear that, despite the twists and turns of life, something magnificent had been retained between them. To witness this was a profound experience. *How could anyone who has seen this settle for less?* I thought.

There are obviously no guarantees in life. We stumble about, get married, have kids, fight, make up, grow apart, grow together. We reach some level of acceptance; we share a home. But is it enough? I thought of my mother when someday, she might be in the same position as Mrs. C. I did not have to close my eyes to picture her with my father's body, to see her face. *Yes,* I thought, *it would be the same.* For all their *stuff,* for their times of stress, for the ways they drive each other crazy, and for their sorrows, my parents still have that *something* between them. They still have the essential kernel of cosmic dust, the spark that ignited them in the first place.

As Mrs. C cared for her husband, it was clear that we were witnessing something holy. In her gentle touch and in her lilting whisper was the reassurance that somewhere, beyond this world, beyond the light that knocks at our windows, beyond our daydream visions, we, too, are held in the invisible arms of the Beloved. We are intimately known—every line on our face, every hair on our head, every crevice of our body—and we are loved. The challenge is to open our eyes and our hearts to this reality. This is especially difficult in times of crisis, when our eyes are dimmed with tears and God seems nowhere to be found.

Where do we begin? Perhaps we begin by doing what we can—by expressing our love and thanks in acts of kindness and compassion. Mrs. C could not bring her husband back to life, but she could bathe him. She could take her suffering and pour it out as tenderness; she could take her grief and transform it back into love. This does not mean that she will be spared the ache of missing her husband or will not have times of loneliness. But when she thinks of his final moments, and of their last moments together, she may find solace in knowing that she did all she could for him, that an act of pure love was performed, and she alone was the one to do it. In remembering, it is possible that she may find a deeper meaning in his passing. If she had died before her husband, who would have been able to do for him what she had done? Perhaps this thought will give her comfort.

In the coming days, I imagine her sitting at the same window, gazing out at the same sun, now warming the buds of spring. In her mind, maybe she will travel across a sparkling blue ocean, feeling the sun on her face and the breeze in her hair. Perhaps I am being presumptuous, but I like to think of her fixing her eyes on the horizon and watching steadily until a rocky shore comes into view. There, she will see a figure waving in the distance. As she draws closer to the shore, she can see that he is smiling. His voice is carried on the breeze, caressing her ears like the warm breath of a whispered secret. His words are for her alone. Later, if asked about them, she will only smile. But in her heart she will hear her husband's voice, calling sweet and clear: "Come to me, my love, when you are ready. Come to me—I will be waiting."

4

SEEING LEO

IN THE ENTRANCE TO a nursing home sits an elderly man in a wheelchair. He is the unofficial greeter, and a notorious flirt. Although he is not a hospice patient, I usually stop to say hello as I pass him on my way to the elevators—elevators that will carry me up to a floor where someone lies dying.

"Hey, Leo!" I say, smiling as I come upon him, pausing to rest my hand on his shoulder. "How are you today?'

Without answering my question, he studies me with his piercing blue eyes. I suddenly feel too tall in my heels, which clip-clop as I walk the bare corridor, and I become acutely aware of the height differential between us. He seems small and far away sitting there, in that chair from which there is no escaping, and I feel awkward as I hover above him. In the momentary pause, I realize that I hadn't expected a conversation when I greeted him, just a friendly hello before moving on.

But he has stopped me with his silence, sizing me up and keeping me there as I wait for his reply.

"You know, you are one hot woman," he says without a hint of irony.

"Gosh, thanks, Leo," I stammer.

"No, I mean it," he presses. "You are really *hot.*"

At that, the security guard at the front desk raises his head sleepily and smiles.

"Wow. Okay, Leo, I'll take it." I laugh lightly, preparing to move on.

But Leo is still looking at me. He is not smiling—he is dead serious. There is something like fire in his eyes, a blue Sterno flame burning in those blue eyes. He is holding me there with the ferocity of his gaze.

"You are so hot, I wish I could just reach up and *grab* you." As he says this, he makes a motion with both of his hands, as if to clutch my rear end.

The guard's eyes widen, and he shakes his head in a silent laugh. But I am not laughing, I am beginning to see; and I realize that I am, perhaps, seeing Leo for the first time. I know that what he is saying is inappropriate. I know that I should tell him so. I think of the nurses and aides who have suffered unwelcome gropes from confused or angry or frustrated patients. The professional in me has every reason to gently scold him and yet . . . I cannot. Instead, I say to him, "Doesn't it stink, Leo, that at this point in your life, at your age, you can't just do what you want? You can't just reach up and grab me?"

"You'd better believe it stinks!" he says, somewhat startled by my response.

"I wish I could let you," I say, "but I can't."

"Yeah, well, what else is new," he grumbles, turning away from me and shoving his chin on his fist. I study him for a moment, then I squat down next to his wheelchair.

"Leo," I say softly, putting my hand on his arm, "I'll bet you had a beautiful wife."

With that, he turns in his chair to face me. This time, my head is tilted up toward his, our faces mere inches apart. Then his expression begins to soften, the anger and hurt dissolving. His eyes become the color of the eastern sky—shimmering, mystical, robin's egg blue.

"I had the most beautiful wife in the world," he whispers, like a secret, with a tenderness that could break your heart. And then he begins to cry. As tears spill down his cheeks, he continues looking at me. He is searching for her in my eyes. He is searching for the reassurance that she existed, that he existed, and that some ember of that life remains, hidden in a place he no longer remembers. Perhaps if he searches long enough, he can find it, rekindle it, feel the warmth of it.

I am perched on the floor, my hand still resting on his arm—and it is as if we are alone, two birds on a wire, suspended between two worlds, neither here nor there. "What was her name?" I ask, after a moment. "How did you meet? What was she like?" Each question prompts the description of a woman and a life that exist now only in memory. Each answer brings Leo a little closer to that life, animating and resuscitating him. He wants me to understand what it was like to be away from her during World War II. He chuckles over the memory of how she would ask him to whisper some of the phrases he had learned while stationed in France. "She loved to hear me speak in French," he says with a sigh. Then, with a little flourish of his hand, he offers up a sample of what he used to say. I'm not sure if he remembers anymore what the phrase means, but it glides from his tongue. He looks at me and smiles, like one who is telling a story to a child, and I am aware that he is keeping the most private and precious parts to himself.

Before my eyes, this man begins to live again. The memory of love infuses him with life and with energy. It oxygenates his blood and brings color to his face. I am aware that I am witnessing the spirit of this man rising from the ashes of his infirmity, rising from the confines of his wheelchair, as if to say: "I am a man, who loved a woman, who lived a life, who was free to walk about just like you. I am a man who is more than this shriveled form you see trapped in a wheelchair, urinating in a diaper, making foolish gestures at young women. I am a man. And I loved a woman. And I love her still. We had a story, and it was a love story. Can anyone hear me?"

Leo tells me his story. And when he is through, I say, "You must miss her very much."

"More than you could know, my dear," he replies, placing his hand gently over mine. "What I would give for just one more night to feel her next to me in bed."

The silence is full between us. It is the silence of moonlight and winter, the silence of the stars burning light-years away, the silence that lives in the middle of the flame. It is not the loud silence of pain but rather the hush beyond the hush of awe, the stillness of connection. After a moment or two, I say, so that only he can hear, "Tonight, when you close your eyes, feel her with you. Closer than close. More than next to you, she is within you. Her love, her smile, the sound of her voice. Feel the comfort of her presence, Leo. She is with you every day and beside you every night."

"Yes, I will do that," he whispers, squeezing my hand in a grandfatherly way. Then, straightening himself in his chair, he says, "Now off you go . . . but come back and see me!"

Before standing, I kiss him lightly on the cheek. Then I straighten up and glide toward the elevators. Looking back at Leo, I am aware that what awaits me on another floor is not someone who is dying but someone who is living, living till the last breath, the last sentence in the story of a life that I will never truly fathom.

5

ZHIVAGO

FOR MY FIFTH BIRTHDAY, I was given the gift of choosing a movie for the family to see. This was a big deal. My parents never went out, money was tight, and movies were special occasion events. In fact, I'm not sure I had ever been to a movie theater before. And so, watching my mother open the newspaper for me was like watching her unwrap some sort of mysterious gift, some treasure map that would lead us to a magical world. It was the summer of 1966. The summer before I started kindergarten, the last summer spent feral and unschooled, unfettered by images of sitting in a row of desks, of feeling self-conscious in my Indian suit, of having to brush my hair on a daily basis, and of spending long hours away from the comfortable freedom of home.

As we were looking over our movie options, my father came into the kitchen and suggested, nonchalantly, that we could always see *Doctor Zhivago. Doctor Zhivago,* the film adaptation of Boris Pasternak's famous novel about the Russian Revolution, staring Omar Sharif and Julie Christie. "Richard!" my mother said with some indignation. "This is your daughter's birthday. That is hardly appropriate."

"Well," he said sheepishly, trying to sound convincing, "I just thought she might enjoy seeing all the horses and the scenery. Besides, it might be a good history lesson."

My mother wasn't biting, but I was hooked—not so much on the promise of horses as on the dawning awareness of my unique position. It was suddenly and strangely within my power to make my father happy. *Doctor Zhivago* had been out for months; I could not have comprehended then how much he must have wanted to see it. He was a struggling writer, a romantic, and a committed father. He and my mother would never have spent the money to go to the movies themselves—and so the prospect of sitting through some animated children's film must have seemed torturous. His only hope was to sufficiently animate the movie poster he had seen, scavenging from it something I loved (horses) and filling in the gaps with what he knew of the story, colored by his own imagination.

"What's it about?" I asked earnestly.

"Well, it is set in Russia during a time of war," my father said in his best storytelling voice. Anything said in that voice was instantly intriguing and immensely exciting. He could have been reading the butcher's daily specials—it didn't matter. When my father was telling a story, the atmosphere changed dramatically, and we were riveted. "And the part that I thought you would especially like," he continued, "is where the doctor is riding through the snow on horseback and all these men are chasing him. The horses are running through the woods, jumping over logs, their breath coming out in puffs of smoke because it is so cold."

"Do any of the horses get hurt?" I asked.

"No. They are very strong and very graceful."

"Okay then," I said with a smile. "I want to see *Doctor Zhivago*."

My mother was furious. She pleaded with me. She assured me that no one (i.e., my father) would be mad at me for choosing a different movie. She reminded me that this was *my* birthday. She showed me enticing advertisements with cartoon princesses. She glared at my father. But I was resolute. I wanted to see *Doctor Zhivago*. The family would see *Doctor Zhivago*.

I remember sitting on my parents' bed as my father called the local theater to check on showtimes. He squeezed my hand and smiled conspiratorially over his black horn-rimmed glasses. I smiled back, giddy with happiness, feeling positively regal in my benevolent exercise of power. I remember the strangeness and the excitement of choosing our seats in the big, old movie theater, of listening to the organist who would play before the movie started, and of watching him disappear into darkness when the lights went down. There were cartoon shorts instead of the endless "coming attractions" that now assault moviegoers with deafening enthusiasm. I snuggled down into the worn, faux velvet seat next to my father, my head against his arm, watched the opening scene, and promptly fell asleep.

The next thing I knew, my dad was gently nudging me

and whispering in my ear, "Look, Andie, horses!" I opened my eyes to see horses, just as he had promised, racing through the snow, beautiful against the backdrop of trees. As I fell back asleep, I fell with the whimsy and the contentment of an autumn leaf drifting on whatever bit of summer was left in the breeze. I fell dancing, I fell swirling; I fell endlessly aloft. The softness of the seat, the smell of the popcorn, the comfort of my father's arm around me, the assurance of my mother's protection, all of these made me sigh deeply and feel ridiculously happy.

Maybe this is why an image from *Doctor Zhivago* comes to me when I am struggling in my life. Clearly, it doesn't matter if we are people of faith, if we have a developed philosophy or are generally happy with our lives; at some time or other, most of us are bound to feel exhausted, lost, or far from home. I've been there on more than one occasion. And when I feel despair, or feel alienated from myself, I go within and search for a memory of being truly happy, of feeling something essential to who I am, something which connects me to the core of my spirit. The memory of my fifth birthday is one that invokes a deep feeling of well-being, of being loved, and of being connected to something greater than myself. It also conjures a particular scene from the movie that I have found helpful in difficult times.

The image is not one I remember from that first viewing, although, ironically, it does involve a horse. It goes something like this: After being conscripted into the Red Army, Omar Sharif's Zhivago has suffered unbelievable hardship. He has seen brutality on every front, he has been elbow-deep in the blood of countless young soldiers, and he is forced to keep moving with the army. He has no idea about the fate of his loved ones, and he is half frozen and starving. The music is like a dirge as the monochromatic scene of bitterness unfolds. Zhivago's horse stops, as if frozen in place, unable or unwilling to go on. Weary soldiers and citizens continue shuffling past him like zombies, moving without reason, moving to keep moving. Nearly indistinguishable from the drifts of snow or the abandoned remains of what must have been a village, the ragged figures move with brute determination into nothingness. Exhausted, broken, he watches them, his eyes as hollow as a dead man's. And then . . . then the palest hint of sun breaks through the sky behind him. He looks over his shoulder, and something comes alive in his eyes. As the last figure staggers past him, the shimmering strains of the balalaika begin to rise—and Zhivago turns his horse toward the sun, toward home, toward life.

In that moment, despite the risk of being shot as a defector, despite the slim possibility of finding his loved ones, Zhivago reaches for life. Perhaps the sun reignited his poet's soul, perhaps the memory of beauty startled him from his frozen tomb, perhaps he was just tired of being cold. In any case, something in Zhivago said *Live,* and he risked everything for that. An alcoholic might call the moments before this "hitting bottom." A religious person might say that he had an epiphany, or that God spoke to him, or that a prayer was answered. However one understands this moment of truth, the experience is one of movement, of a burning desire to turn toward home—or whatever it is that symbolizes the alleviation of suffering, the will to live, the possibility of peace.

Most of us have had our versions of sitting on that horse, miserable, battered, sick and tired of the path we are on. What could make us stop and turn the other way? What might give us the courage to risk change, to feel again that we need not suffer so? The Buddha spoke of the Four Noble Truths. Roughly paraphrased, they are: Life is suffering; the suffering is my own doing; life does not have to be suffering; I've suffered enough.* Sometimes things happen that are beyond our control—these may involve illness, death, the loss of a job or a relationship—but we always have within our power the way in which we face them. When we forget to see beauty, we are lost. When we no longer believe that we are loved, we are lost. When we cease to hear the Muse whispering in our ears, we are lost. When we forget who we are, we are lost. It is up to each one of us to decide how much suffering is enough, and to begin our journey toward life and love and peace.

In her book *Radical Acceptance,* Tara Brach, Buddhist teacher and author, tells the story of a white tiger named Mohini. She writes:

Mohini was a regal white tiger who lived for many years at the Washington, D.C. National Zoo. For most of those years her home was in the old lion house—a typical twelve-by-twelve-foot cage with iron bars and a cement floor. Mohini spent her days

* Dr. John Diamond beautifully summarizes the Four Noble Truths in his book *Life-Energy Analysis: A Way to Cantillation* (Ridgefield, Conn.: Enhancement Books, 1988). His influence on my understanding of these cannot be measured, and I am grateful.

pacing restlessly back and forth in her cramped quarters. Eventually, biologists and staff worked together to create a natural habitat for her. Covering several acres, it had hills, trees, a pond and a variety of vegetation. With excitement and anticipation they released Mohini into her new and expansive environment. But it was too late. The tiger immediately sought refuge in a corner of the compound, where she lived for the remainder of her life. Mohini paced and paced in that corner until an area twelve by twelve feet was worn bare of grass.[†]

WHEN I HEARD this story, it terrified me. Mohini was the anti-Zhivago. I could be Zhivago or I could be Mohini—which would it be? I realized that being rescued from circumstances with which I was struggling did not mean that I would know freedom. I could very well stick to my old patterns, my old ways of coping, without ever recognizing that I need not suffer so, that the bars on my life were largely imaginary and of my own making. Early on, Mohini probably longed for freedom, for relief from her suffering, but then something happened. Perhaps she forgot who she was. Did she go crazy in captivity? Did she become so accustomed to being the pacing shell of a tiger that she was paralyzed when set free? And how would it have been different if she had achieved the freedom herself, in some spectacular force of will, breaking free from her captivity on her own?

[†]Tara Brach, *Radical Acceptance: Embracing Your Life with the Heart of a Buddha* (New York: Bantam Books, 2003), pp. 24–25.

Perhaps this is part of the secret. Our release from suffering has to come from within. It cannot be granted from some benevolent power; it cannot be handed to us like a winning lotto ticket. True peace can only be achieved when the individual decides to make that spiritual move, when the heart is suddenly stirred to open, when the soul catches fire from a spark of inspiration, when we remember who we are. Then, no external circumstance can limit where the spirit will wander.

I wonder sometimes if those of us who pray for help really want it: Do we truly want to change? Or do we ask for guidance, for direction, and then stick our fingers in our ears? Afraid, immobilized, I am Mohini; opening my heart, I aspire to be Zhivago. Opening my heart, I can hear the Voice which is ever there to guide me. Whether I follow it is my choice, each moment and at every turn.

Sometimes this Voice emanates from the throat of a stranger. Sometimes it speaks in the language of nature. Sometimes it comes as memory. I have recognized it in the stubborn courage of those who face tragedy—and in those making peace with death. And when I was diagnosed with breast cancer, that familiar Voice guided me through the perilous journey of surgery, chemotherapy, and the beginnings of recovery. The same Voice that was with me in childhood calls to me now. We all know it, we've all heard it. It is as near and familiar as the soft lilt of the Mother calling us home to dinner.

We each are called by name. We are each known and loved and cared for. Listening doesn't mean that we will be spared hardship; it means that we will know the comfort and the reassurance that we are not alone.

6

NO OTHER HANDS

WHEN I WAS A child, I believed that God was as near as the exhalation of my breath. God was all around me, an invisible plasma in which I floated and moved. God could hear me when I prayed, He could see me when I aspired to do good or when I acted miserably. God was, in fact, a little scary. I believed He could and would punish bad behavior (nothing personal), but could also grant amazing gifts, like finding a robin's nest or seeing a shooting star. God was as real and as looming as the face of the man in the moon—a presence from whom you could not run but whose face was occasionally hidden. And just when I would wonder, *Where are you, God? Where are you now?* I would gaze at the trees swaying lazily in the summer breeze and sense that God was waving to me, saying, "Here I am. I am right here. How ya doin'?"

This idea of God as an active participant in my life—a God who was part spectator, part judge, and part lifeguard—

was going along pretty well in those early years. I could accept God spying on me from his place in the sky. It was not a bad bargain. I did my part by praying, by behaving, and by remembering to acknowledge the beauty of creation, and God essentially left me alone (unless I was in trouble).

Our unspoken agreement was solidified one summer when my sister and I almost managed to drown ourselves in our swimming pool in an act of bravado and stupidity. I was eight and she was nine. The pool had just been drained and cleaned for the summer, and we were participating in the annual torture of waiting for it to fill with water. Even in Ohio, with little else to do, we tired of sitting and watching one small garden hose battle the abyss of an empty pool. It was hot, and we were bored, and we convinced ourselves that one quick dip wouldn't hurt anybody. If we were caught going in without permission, it was certain punishment; but who would know, we reckoned, who would know?

Just one quick dip. One swim to the other side and we're out. That was the plan. We hopped into the empty shallow end and slid into the water of the deep. Trouble was, once we swam to the deep end of the pool, we could not reach the side. The water was over our heads but too low for us to be able to grasp the edge of the pool. For some reason, the shallow end looked so far away—and we weren't sure whether we could get back up the slippery slope that had been so much fun going down. And so we panicked. We were like two little oyster crackers stuck in the soup. We tried everything imaginable to get ourselves out of there. We tried springing off the bottom; we tried boosting each other up; we treaded water.

Soon we realized there was a real possibility that we might both drown. The dilemma was this: Should we yell for our father, who was just inside the house, knowing we would be in big trouble, or should we just take our punishment and drown?

After what seemed like an eternity, we chose to yell, and out came our dad. I can still see him clearly in my mind, bursting through the back door with his dark hair, his black horn-rimmed glasses, and his adrenaline pumping. In one swift move, he reached down and pulled us simultaneously out of the pool like two sinking buckets. *We're saved!* I thought. *Too bad we're dead.*

Trembling, with rubbery legs and beating hearts, we fully expected a very stern rebuke. Instead, Dad held our two wet bodies close to him, kissing one and then the other, his voice gentle and reassuring. "You did the right thing to call for me," he said. "Never be afraid. I am always here. I am always within the sound of your voice."

That was God for me in 1969. God was the one who would always hear. God would come if you called. God would rescue, even if you did something stupid. God was the strong arms that loved and forgave you.

That wasn't the God I met a year later.

On an impossibly blue November day, my family was picnicking with our closest friends. We were all together in the country when the youngest child of our friends, six-year-old Matthew, started screaming that he had a headache. We all thought—the children, that is—that he might have touched the electric fence we'd been flirting with. The adults quickly packed up the picnic, piled us into the station wagon, and headed for home.

I was sitting in the "way back" of the station wagon with my sister, my five-year-old brother, and Matthew's brother, Tim, who was ten. Matthew was lying across his mother's lap in the backseat, with my mother next to her. As we drove, it was beginning to get dark. Matthew stopped crying, and the car was filled with the soft, soothing voices of adults trying to get everyone home. But when we arrived at their house and his mother carried him inside, we discovered Matthew wasn't sleeping, he was in a coma.

I remember sitting in the back of the station wagon as his mother burst through her front door, screaming for her oldest son, an Eagle Scout, to administer CPR. I remember watching in shock as an ambulance arrived and took them away. And finally, I remember my mother waking us in the morning with tears in her eyes, trying to explain how Mattie had died of a brain aneurysm in the middle of the night.

Sometimes I see it all in slow motion—the blue of the sky, the electric fence, Timmy standing with a stick in his hand, Mattie's blue eyes, my little brother smiling, my sister sitting in the grass. Then the screaming—Mattie holding his head, the ride home, the agonized cry for help, the ambulance. I play it over and over, thinking that maybe I got it wrong. Maybe I am not remembering it quite right. Maybe it is all a dream and Matthew is now a forty-five-year-old man who is happily married with three children. But I know it is not so.

Where was God? I wondered. *Where was God for Mattie? Where were the ears that heard, the eyes that saw?* I knew that I

was no better a child than he. He had done nothing wrong—
he hadn't even done anything stupid. And yet, God did not
come bursting through to save him. There were no strong
arms, no words of reassurance. There was only this small white
coffin and a wake of shattered hearts.

Thus began my journey toward an acceptance of the unex-
plainable and the tragic. Life is not clear-cut; belief in God is
not easy. Children live and children die. Hardships happen.
We get sick. We have accidents. We are damaged beyond re-
pair. We are essentially left to our own devices. What possible
relevance could a belief in God have when it seems that God is
only vaguely concerned, quixotic and random in his mercy? I,
for one, wanted no part of that God—but I was terrified to
ditch the idea altogether.

What I have come to understand is that the events that
happen to us and to those we love have no bearing on God's
love for us. One of my grandmothers, for example, died at the
age of 34, when my father was 9, the other at 106. Was one
more loved, more cherished? Was one a better person? The idea
is absurd. And yet a part of me still believes we can ensure pros-
perity and health by our piety. In reality, the only thing we can
ever control is how we cope with what befalls us.

Through the years, I have continued to see God in the
waving trees, and occasionally in the face of the moon, but I
also recognize the Holy in the love and compassion of ordinary people. I think of my mother, how she carried her friend's
grief, how she was there day after day, bringing food, bringing
friendship, mothering the children who had lost a brother, and
whose mother was bereft. I think of the courage of Mattie's

mother, and his father and brothers, in the face of that terrible loss—a loss from which there would never be full recovery. Like learning to live without a limb, without an essential part of oneself, those who grieve the loss of a loved one must learn again how to be in the world. "Who are we without this one whom we loved?" they ask. "How do we go on?"

How? As trite as it sounds, one day at a time. Slowly. Sometimes cursing, sometimes crying, sometimes laughing so hard at a memory that grief is held at bay for a moment or two. We make peace with our regrets. We try to forgive. We tell the stories over and over until the edges are polished—smooth as sea glass, tumbled through time. In the end, we remember to keep breathing. We curl ourselves in the palm of God's hand and rest, for that is where we always are anyway. Held and loved.

I don't know why I didn't drown in that pool, but I know it had nothing to do with being good. This is what I try to bring to those who are experiencing the pain of losing someone they love. There are no easy answers. Perhaps the best we can do is to keep calling out, keep believing that there is One who hears, and to be open to the ways in which God comes to us. As the German theologian Dorothee Sölle wrote: "God has no other hands than ours." When our hearts are willing to break for another person, and our hands are willing to hold another in love, then something profound can transpire—the awareness of grace, the experience of genuine compassion, the incarnation of Hope.

7

ARE YOU THE ONE?

*We may wonder whom can I love and serve? Where is
the face of God to whom I can pray?
The answer is simple. That naked one. That lonely one.
That unwanted one is my brother and my sister. If we
have no peace, it is because we have forgotten that we
belong to each other.*
—Mother Teresa

Approaching the Pine Street Inn, Boston's largest shelter for the homeless, I took a deep breath. The long walk down the alleyway leading to the entrance was already lined with a hundred huddled men waiting to be let inside. It was bitter cold, and they stood along the wall shifting from one foot to the other, some smoking, some in animated discussions, others talking to themselves, all waiting for the doors to open. No matter how many times I did it, it always felt like walking the gauntlet. I would smile, trying to look relaxed, grateful to see a familiar face or two, but I was also uncomfortably aware of the eyes upon me, eyes that were curious, hungry, desperate, defiant. I never felt endangered, but I felt something close to being invaded, though not a hand ever touched me.

What am I doing here? I would ask myself in those first few months. I was a first-year divinity student at Harvard, twenty-two years old, and had chosen the Pine Street Inn as a field education placement. I was given a small stipend to serve as an extra pair of hands for the staff there, which could mean handing out clothing or bed tickets, assisting the older gentlemen with their dinner, or just being present to listen to the many stories of those we called guests of the Inn.

Each afternoon, especially as the weather turned colder, the men would line up in the alleyway. The first 350 to enter would receive a bed ticket; the remaining few hundred would have to make do on the floor. And so they lined up early to ensure themselves a bed, a shower, a place in the food line, even though it meant standing sometimes for hours in the cold. So much of life at the Inn was about lines: There was a line to get in, a line for a bed ticket, a line for food, for medicine, for clothing. It required either extraordinary patience or sheer resignation, depending on point of view.

At 3:30, the doors would open, and the Inn would come alive. It was an incredibly chaotic time, with hundreds of men passing through the doors in a variety of physical and mental states. A police officer stood by every afternoon to frisk each man who entered for weapons or alcohol. This was a necessary indignity suffered by old and young alike to ensure something close to safety. Obviously it could not eliminate fights or injuries entirely, but it helped. Some nights the stream of broken humanity seemed endless—and I would wonder at the ability of the small staff to meet so many needs, handle so many problems, and keep the lines flowing.

On this particular night, the police brought in a man they had plucked off the streets. This happened frequently in the winter. Making their rounds, the police would come across someone who had passed out, half frozen in the cold, and bring him to Pine Street. I remember being behind the front desk handing out bed tickets when there was some commotion at the door. It was the sound of walkie-talkies and the authoritative voices of police officers instructing people to make way. I glanced up as two officers came in supporting a small clump of a man whose legs were dragging behind him. They nodded to their colleague who was stationed at the door. The flash of their eyes and their pure vitality provided a dramatic contrast to the other men who were entering those same doors in an endless stream of tattered humanity.

"This one's got no ID," one of the officers shouted to whoever was close enough to hear. "He's drunk as a skunk. Maybe someone can get a name or an address out of him."

With that, they plopped him in a chair, waved good-bye to the cop at the door, and disappeared into the alleyway.

The social worker sitting next to me let out something between a groan and a sigh. She had the focused tension of a factory line worker who was moving as fast and efficiently as she could. To pause from her work might throw the whole line off; and so she turned to me and said, "Hey, Andie, try to get a name out of that guy, okay?" With that, she returned to her work and didn't look back.

I slid off my stool behind the desk and walked around to where the man was sitting. It was just barely out of the path of the entryway, the path of the lines streaming by for beds and food and medication. As I squatted down by his metal folding chair, the men passing by would occasionally bump me, and I would have to hold on as if to keep myself from being swept away in the current. But there, from my perch on the floor, I began to take him in.

He was a slight man with watery blue eyes and the leathery skin of one who had spent far too many days and nights outside. He could have been fifty, but he looked seventy. His clothes were dirty and smelled of the street, of urine and vomit, and God knows what else. He had a little blue beanie perched toward the back of his head, which gave him the look of a sailor, like Popeye's old, drunken pappy or disgraced uncle. Drooling slightly, and careening to one side, he was coming dangerously close to falling off his chair; so I steadied him and took his rough hand. It was cracked and swollen, with long, yellow nails, and it bore the scrapes of countless forgotten falls.

"Can you give me your name, sir?" I asked, looking up at him.

He mumbled something unintelligible, something which sounded nothing like a name.

I tried again. "Sir, what is your name? Can you tell me?"

More mumbles, but this time, perhaps a clue. Straining to make out the sounds in the midst of all the chaos, I leaned closer to his face—or did he lean closer to mine as he swayed from the chair?

"Was that George? John? Jim?" I asked.

Still nothing from him that I could understand, nothing that came close to a name. We sat there a few minutes more, I on my knees on the floor, he on the edge of his metal chair, men passing by. I started wondering what else I could do—and then he raised his eyes to mine and looked directly at me as if seeing me there for the first time. Then he said with startling clarity, "Are you the one God sent to me? Are you the one?"

Those words nearly knocked me off my knees. The power of them, the vibration of them, the shock of their clear enunciation. "Are you the one?" What was I to do with that? In a millisecond, I was both amazed at his sudden ability to articulate and panicked at how I should respond. But before I could answer, he continued.

"Because if you're the one God sent to me, then God sent me to you." Whispering now and with intensity, he repeated, "Then God sent me to *you*."

After that, not another discernible word was uttered by this nameless, homeless man. He shut his eyes and resumed his unintelligible mumbles, and I knelt there stunned, bathed in silence, and momentarily unaware of anything else happening around me.

"Did you get a name?" asked the social worker as she hurried by, breaking the trance.

"No . . . no," I said softly, knowing I could never explain what had just happened.

"That's okay. I think we're gonna get him to Mass General

for detox. We need you to help with dinner now. Ernie, move this guy, would you? He's gonna fall off that chair and crack his head open."

I hesitated, unable to tear myself away from him. Then the social worker said with genuine compassion, "It's okay, Andie. We'll take care of him. There are others who need your help now."

As I made my way back to Cambridge that night, back through the hallowed halls of Harvard Yard, back to the warmth of my little room, back to studying about God, talking about God, thinking about God, dissecting God, I knew that I had glimpsed God in the eyes of this man. And I finally realized what I was doing at Pine Street, what I was doing in divinity school. It was not just to help those who needed help; it was not to be some sort of do-gooder. It was to save my own life, my own soul. I needed to be there. I needed to be among the broken, among the outcast and the despised. God was sending them to me as if to say, "Remember who you are. Remember who I am. You will never find me in the ancient texts, in hermeneutics or exegesis, in theology or philosophy if you cannot see me in my people."

I never saw that man again, never knew what happened to him—but I carry him with me every day. I carry his bruises, his cracked nails, his soiled clothes. I carry the light that flashed in his eyes momentarily like lightning, startling me with the power of its truth. If I was sent to him to offer love and compassion, then he was sent to me to remind me that we are not separate from one another, we are not more important, more worthy of love. Where do we find God? We find God exactly in the interface of two hearts meeting, just at the point of intersection when we open our eyes to one another, when we dare to see the other as the one sent to us.

When I start to forget, I summon this man; I see his eyes and hear his voice. The lesson he taught me carried me through divinity school. Without him, I might have seen God only through the lens of academia; with him, I found myself, found a deeper understanding of the Holy, and eventually found meaning through working with the battered, the dying, and those suffering incredible hardship. Not all of us need to put ourselves in places of pain and suffering to encounter the Divine, but it is a fertile place to start. What we must remember is that, wherever we find ourselves, whatever door at which we stand knocking, we may encounter something like holiness, something like an angel wrapped in tattered clothes, if only we pause to listen.

8

GIRL IN THE CLOUDS

IT WAS TWO DAYS before Thanksgiving. Grocery stores were hopping, bakeries were churning out pumpkin pies and apple pies and cookies with Pilgrim hats; people scurried about making preparations for visitors, while schoolchildren sang earnestly about being grateful. The time of the harvest was at hand, and it was colored brown and orange—autumn's last hurrah before surrendering to the monochromatic brushstroke of winter. More than ever before, I felt the nearness of that chill. Driving south on the parkway, I noticed a few leaves still clinging stubbornly to their branches—but mostly the trees stretched their bare arms toward the sky, like interlocking black lace, in an act of delicate defiance. "What more do you want from me?" they seemed to shrug, hands uplifted, gesturing toward the god of changing seasons. "My leaves are gone, but I stand here still, ready to bear the coming winter. We've done this dance a time or two before."

Perhaps I heard the whispers of the trees because I needed something to hold on to, something to remind me of the on-goingness of time and life, of the seasons and eternity and the way in which living things change form, disappear, die, and are reborn as green shoot, as sapling, as butterfly and lion cub. I was heading to a home where a child was dying to give support to a family standing on the abyss of heartbreak. It was inconceivable. Clearly there were no words that could comfort. The table would have an empty place, and there was nothing for me to offer except my own outstretched arms, my own barren anguish.

This child, this little girl, was about the age of my own daughter—eight years old—when she came onto our hospice program with a recurring brain tumor. Her name was Lila, and she was as delicate and as beautiful as that name implies. She had a head of fine golden hair and large, searching eyes and limbs of creamy satin cord. She had been through an unbear-able amount of suffering, involving more treatments, more disappointments than anyone with any faith could reasonably accept. I visited Lila and her family regularly over the several months that she was on hospice. When I left her, I would gaze upon her sleeping face, fairy hair strewn whimsically across her pillow, and a part of me would crack—the bow of my boat, perhaps, that which keeps me afloat, keeps me from lurching and rolling when the winds pick up and the seas grow rough. My heart would heave and groan with the senselessness of it all, with the grief and the sorrow, and with the inability to turn that boat around. And I would struggle with what could possibly help this child and her family to bear the storm, the brutal coming winter.

Now, Lila was dying. There was no more controlling symptoms, no more last hopes, however faint. When I got the word, I jumped in my car and headed down the parkway in the direction from which I had just come. It was late in the afternoon, and my usual workday had already finished. I suppose I said good-bye to my kids, got them settled with dinner and homework, and explained to my husband that I had an emergency. It is a blur to me now. But that ride to Lila's house remains strangely clear—the trees silhouetted against the sky, the rush-hour cars pressing for position, and the sun starting to streak orange-red across the horizon.

I glanced up at the changing sky as I drove, searching without words for something I could not name. Was it reassurance? Inspiration? Wisdom? Then something caught my eye, startling me with its presence. There, above me, running alongside and ahead of me, was the most perfectly formed cloud I had ever seen. It was in the exact shape of a little girl in a dress, arms outstretched, legs running, hair flowing behind her. "Lila!" I whispered.

For some reason, I happened to have a disposable camera with me. Driving with one hand, I fumbled in my bag with the other. I was so struck with the image that I felt a desperate urge to record it and to preserve it. I was afraid I would never be able to adequately describe what I was seeing. Who could believe it? The sky was changing rapidly now. My girl in the clouds was chasing the setting sun, dissolving into the river of fire gold flowing above me. I managed to get off two shots through my rather grimy windshield; then I placed the camera on the seat next to me and focused on the road ahead. *Was*

Lila gone? I wondered. Was that the manifestation of her spirit, the angel imprint of her release—or was it a sign of the freedom to come, the playmate waiting to run with her?

Maybe I put more stock in the clouds than most. Maybe I read into things a little too much; but it is part of my conditioning, part of my makeup. When I was a child, I would sometimes lie with my face in the earth, digging into the soft, fragrant dirt, making gloves of the grass between my fingers. I would breathe deeply, inhaling the green life, the chlorophyll and minerals, the infusion of sun and rain and tunneling worms and molten lava buried miles and miles below. *I love this earth and the earth loves me,* I would think, smiling as I held on, feeling the spinning revolutions that fixed me to that spot, where shoots of life passed from the ground through my rib cage and upward to the sun. After a time, I would roll over onto my back and look up at the sky that was looking at me. Somehow, it didn't seem so far away. Clouds would pass like smoke signals from the heavens, sending messages encoded for my private viewing. "Yes, yes," I would say, conspiratorially, as they floated by. I imagined that, if I let go of the grass, I would fly up to them, released from gravity, and would be able to ride the horse, the dragon, the hawk that had come for me.

It had always seemed to be this way for me. Even when I was in college, I would sometimes lie on the ground and contemplate the sky. In the first weeks of my senior year, I remember walking down the concrete steps that led through a small patch of woods separating the upper and lower campuses. It was a perfect September day, and I felt completely happy to be alive—to be there, in that moment, twenty-one years old, in a world pulsating with life and energy and possibility. I paused halfway down the steps, wanting to linger for a moment in the shady quiet of that in-between space. Plopping down on a little landing, I decided to stretch out, tucking a book beneath my head for a pillow. There, I took in the leaves shimmering high above me, the rays of sunlight dancing between the branches as they swayed in the breeze, the sounds of chirping birds and squirrels scampering by, and the echo of voices from what seemed like very far away.

After a while, my eyes happened to rest on one particular leaf some forty feet above me. For several minutes, I watched it wave and flutter, breathing in unison with the breath that moved the branches. Then, to my surprise, the leaf came free!—I witnessed the very moment it left the tree—and I let out a little sigh of exclamation. I don't think I had ever seen that particular moment of surrender in quite the same way before. Obviously I had seen leaves falling every autumn of my life, but never so specifically, so individually. I lay there still as a stone as it made its descent. My right hand was resting close to my head, my left was at my side. The leaf twirled gracefully in the breeze, floating this way and that, far above me. I watched, motionless, as it made its way down, closer and closer, dancing to nature's secret melody.

Slowly, I uncurled my fingers—and there, into the center of my open palm, near my cheek, landed the leaf. A kiss from the tree. "Thank you," I said out loud. My cells continued to vibrate at the speed required to keep me solid, to keep up the pretense of being separate from everything else, from the leaf and the tree and even that hard concrete—but in my heart, I knew we were one. Shutting my eyes, the leaf still in my hand, I lay there for some time, lost to the experience of mystery and unity. Finally, sensing the shadow of a presence, I opened my eyes and nearly gave the student standing over me a heart attack.

"Oh my God! I thought you were dead!" exclaimed a jean-clad boy, jumping backward. I laughed, realizing how it must have looked: a motionless girl sprawled across the steps in the middle of the woods, books strewn carelessly aside. "Are you okay? Did you pass out or something?" he asked, with a mixture of curiosity and concern.

"No." I smiled, sitting up. "I was just zoning for a minute." How could I explain that I had had a mystical experience?

"All right. Whatever." He shrugged, stepping past me. I watched him bound down the steps; then I tucked the leaf into a book and continued my own descent.

The impulse to look up whenever I stepped outside was rooted in the expectation that, at any moment, I might receive a greeting from the Beyond in the form of clouds, or waving trees, or the face in the moon. The natural world was very alive—and not only was it mystical but it wanted to communicate its mysteries with whoever was willing to listen. Because of this, I never felt alone. I was being accompanied by a host of spiritual entities who were doing their best to help me hear and see them.

This was never more clear than when I was about ten. I remember coming through the sliding glass doors that led into our backyard. It was summer, and the late afternoon was stretching and yawning its way into evening. I stood for a moment on the little concrete patio, enjoying the way it felt warm and smooth beneath my bare feet. My father had just cut the grass, and the air was fragrant with green and with honeysuckle and with some neighbor's barbecue. I watched my mother casually pace the edge of our pool as my brother and sister swam; she paused now and then to pull a weed from along the fence.

I raised my eyes to the sky, a Wagnerian blue—mystical, impossible. And there, to my surprise, I saw the body of a man floating slowly toward the heavens. He was naked and rather emaciated looking. His posture indicated that he was being held like a baby in arms I could not see. I noticed he looked somewhat startled, afraid even, but not terrified. I did not know what surrender looked like, but I can say now his expression was something like that. I looked around at my family, at my father and mother. Did anyone else see him? I wanted to speak or to run up to them, but I was riveted to that spot. Then recognition began to dawn. I studied his face again and realized that he looked like the father of my friend Karen. Could it be? He had always seemed rather frail, but it never would have occurred to me then that he might be dying.

The pastoral serenity of the scene on the ground continued without a ripple—but I felt myself neither here nor there. I could neither call out to my parents to look up at the sky nor communicate with the vision before me. I could only stand there looking toward the heavens. Slowly, I began to see many figures rising in still more invisible arms. They were steadily appearing now, as if popping into the atmosphere like fireworks. Though I could not see them, I intuited the presence of spiritual beings carrying these people. The feeling was one of great compassion and tenderness. Some people's expressions, I observed, were peaceful. Some were like the first man I saw—anxious. All of them were rising like helium balloons at different heights, different speeds, each one disappearing into the blue, blue twilight sky.

Finally, the vision faded and I approached my father. "Dad," I said, "I think I just saw Karen's father being taken into heaven. Did you see anything?" My father leaned on the rake he had been using; a soft pile of grass clippings lay fresh and moist at his feet. He studied me for a moment with interest, then scanned the horizon as if fully expecting to see someone floating there.

"I guess I was too busy with the grass," he said thoughtfully. "But tell me what you saw."

I described to him the scene that had unfolded in front of me. He nodded, listening intently, his eyes igniting and crackling like fire, as they always did whenever the mystical made an unexpected visit. Resting his hand on my shoulder, he looked upward again. We stood like that for a few minutes as the first evening stars began to appear. There was nothing more to say. We took it for granted that my experience had been authentic.

The next day, I learned that my friend's father had in fact died. Although he had been a heavy smoker, and always seemed to suffer from a cough, everyone said that his death was rather sudden. He had not been a religious man, which might explain why his expression struck me as a little tentative. I never told my friend what I had seen—and, as the years passed, I often wondered if I had been dreaming, if I had dreamt the whole thing up. Were it not for the smell of that grass and the sound of my brother and sister in the pool, and the concrete beneath my feet, I might have forgotten that it was real.

And so, when I saw the girl in the clouds, I saw with the eyes of my childhood, eyes that were accustomed to receiving such messages, even if I didn't fully understand them. The only uncertainty this time was whether the child to whom I was driving was still alive—and that would be answered soon enough.

When I arrived at the house, Lila was surrounded by her mother and father, and by the hospice nurse and doctor. She was alive, but just barely, resting comfortably in her parents' bed. There was little for me to do. I said a prayer, I stroked her head; I offered words of what I hoped to be comfort. I watched the nurse and doctor work, speaking in hushed tones, brows furrowed, (clearly) trying to ease the child's discomfort and to buy a little more time. After a while, I left, got into my car, and headed back up the parkway—only this time, there was no girl in the clouds, no sky of fire. Perhaps she was hiding just beyond the haze that blocked the stars, or maybe she had dispersed into the atmosphere—re-forming, shifting, preparing to descend now as dew. The idea of having her a bit closer heartened me, but I knew, even then, that she would pass through my hands, ephemeral, elusive, beyond my grasp.

The next day, I learned of Lila's death. The dew had evaporated by then and there were no clouds in the sky, nothing to ease the sense of loss and distance. I was to meet the family at the funeral home to offer support and perhaps a blessing over Lila's body. When I arrived, however, I was told that there had been an emergency, that someone in the family had become overwhelmed with grief and needed to be taken to the hospital. They were going to be delayed indefinitely. "Would you like to offer her a blessing?" asked the funeral director gently. "I told the family you were coming, and I think it would give them comfort to know you had blessed her." "Of course," I answered, drawing a deep breath. "Of course."

He led me downstairs into a room I had never seen, although I had presided over many, many funerals there. It was the room in which bodies were prepared for embalming or for simple burial. The child had arrived just an hour or so before me. She was lying on a steel table, covered to her bare shoulders in a white sheet, a towel folded neatly beneath her head. Her eyes were closed, and her hair spilled in soft, golden waves against the makeshift pillow. She looked exactly like a sleeping princess. I pulled a chair over and sat beside her, my hand resting lightly on her head. It was nearly impossible to believe that she was dead. Nearly impossible. I didn't try to stem the tears that flowed down my cheeks. There was no point. Instead, I looked at her face, serene now, unfurrowed and free from pain. That much was clear. Then I bowed my head and prayed . . . prayed for her mother and father and brothers, prayed that the river of grief would not consume them entirely and that they would have friends and loved ones to help ease the burden for them. And I prayed for Lila, asking the girl in the clouds to take her hand and to guide her on her journey, hoping that she was dancing now, free from needles and pain, and free from a body that had grown weary long before its time. I kissed her on the forehead and smoothed her hair—then I forced myself to leave.

Once again I found myself on the parkway, this time heading toward my own children, who were eagerly anticipating Thanksgiving vacation in Ohio with their aunts and uncles, grandparents and cousins. My heart was so heavy, I could barely feign the enthusiasm expected by my children. It was going to be a long drive.

For the first hour or so, I busied myself with calls—to the family, to their priest—helping in a small way to coordinate plans for the funeral service. Then I stared out my window as the scenery passed, lost in the wordless heartache of what could never be fixed. I looked to the heavens, yes, for that is what I do—but I did not expect to find the girl in the clouds, or any sign, really. Sometimes the Cosmos itself remains silent in reverential respect for human suffering. This silence is often misinterpreted as indifference or even banal cruelty. But what could be crueler than hasty reassurance when all one feels is the desperate need to cry out, to shake one's fist at the glorious sunset, to rant like a madman, hurling oneself against the very mist that has spirited life away?

It is a large breast we beat against—and we can pound and cry and curse and despair until our sobs subside and the ragged hiccups that tear at our breath finally rock us into exhausted sleep. Then, perhaps, in days to come, when we are least expecting it, the heavens will rend and bear a beam of light, and it will take the shape of hope and of the indescribable knowledge that we are loved. This experience will trigger a spontaneous, nonsensical Yes to life—the affirmation that we are one with all creation, and that our journey here is but a short stint on a parkway that bends and dips, rises and falls, leading us ever on toward freedom and reunion. We cannot be abandoned by the stars. The moon does not turn its face from us. The trees do not surrender strength or beauty when they drop their leaves. And we do not cease to be God's children when we suffer or when we doubt, or when the storms of winter come with biting force. Even if all is stripped away, one thing at last remains: the everyday blessedness embodied in creation, the secret of our belovedness, whispered from Soul to Soul.

9

GETTING THERE

L IKE MOST PEOPLE, I can remember exactly where I was
on September 11, 2001. I was in the middle of morning up-
date at the Jansen Memorial Hospice in Tuckahoe, New York,
where I served as chaplain and pastoral care coordinator. Each
morning, at 8:30, we would gather to hear the report from the
night before, learning who had died, who had had difficulty
in the night, and who was currently in distress. Based on the
report, we would triage, form our plans for the day, and then
begin to move out into the community to care for the patients
and families on our program.

In the midst of this familiar routine, our office manager,
Evelyn, rushed in to inform us that a plane had hit the World
Trade Center. We were stunned but assumed it to be a small
private plane, one that had wandered off course. "Keep us
posted," we told Evelyn with concern; then we went on with

the report. Fifteen minutes later, she rushed in again, saying, "Another plane just hit the other tower!"

"Oh my God," said one of the social workers, "we're at war."

I remember thinking that this was a bit dramatic, but everything started spinning. We didn't have access to a TV, so we told Evelyn to bring in the radio. I ran to my desk to call my husband, who happened to be home that morning, and told him to turn on the television. I also instinctively called my parents in Indiana to let them know I was okay. I knew they would worry, even though I worked in Westchester, a good thirty minutes from the World Trade Center. My mother was relieved to hear my voice. "I knew you probably wouldn't be in the city this morning, but I'm so glad to hear from you." I could feel her concern and the fears with which she quietly struggles over having a child so far away, especially in this increasingly unpredictable world.

"I'm okay, Mom," I said. "I knew you would be worried. I'd better go, but I'll call you later."

I returned to the conference room, where the hospice team was listening to the radio and starting to form an emergency plan. This was before the towers fell, before we could grasp the scope of the nightmare. The patients who most needed to be seen would be seen. Those who could wait, or who could manage with a phone call, would be put off until tomorrow. After those with the most acute needs were attended to, all team members were to report back to the office. The thinking was that we should be ready to lend support to the local hospital. In those first hours, we fully anticipated a flood of wounded people coming in through the Lawrence Hospital emergency room in Bronxville, New York. Lawrence would be one of the closest Westchester hospitals available in the event that the city hospitals were overrun. And so we waited.

The towers fell. My husband watched in horror as the unthinkable transpired on the television. He said he was screaming as the first tower collapsed—and again as the second one folded like a house of cards. Then he rode his bike to one of the piers in Rye, where he could see the smoke billowing from across Long Island Sound. I paced the office ten miles away, torn between professional commitment and maternal instinct. I was prepared to assist with the wounded and dying, and felt called to do so if necessary, but I was also fighting a frantic desire to gather my children to me, to feel them and smell them and make sure they were safe. I thought of my mother—and, of course, I thought of the mothers who would not get a call, the ones who would be waiting and waiting for the dear voice that would never come. Finally, just before 3:00, I got in my car and headed back up to Rye. I knew there were clergy of every denomination within walking distance of the local hospital. And, as it would turn out, no wounded ever came.

I arrived at my children's elementary school just in time for pickup. Mothers were standing on the playground quietly asking about each other's husbands. Some were crying, others embracing. Everyone was trying to confirm whose husband worked in or near the towers and whose did not. The school had decided not to tell the children anything about the attack.

The prevailing wisdom was that parents should have the opportunity to explain it to their own children.

That evening, planes circled endlessly overhead. They roared over our house in loud bursts. I didn't know whether to feel protected or scared out of my mind. My husband and I sat with our two children, ages five and eight, to discuss what had happened. They nodded solemnly, clearly unable to grasp it. Who of us could? All of us were reaching for straws, for anything that might make sense of this heinously senseless act. Thinking it might help, we asked our eight-year-old daughter if she wanted to stay up with us and watch President Bush's first address to the nation. We thought she might find comfort in seeing that the country was not in chaos, and that someone was in charge. But when we asked her if she wanted to do this, she looked up at us earnestly and said, "But Mommy, we think President Bush is an idiot."

I stammered a bit and managed to explain, "Well, uh, yes, we don't agree with most of his policies, but he is in charge right now, and we need to pray for him. We need to pray that God gives him the wisdom to lead our country through this terrible time."

She nodded in agreement. "Okay, Mommy. I can do that. Let's watch."

Later that night, a loud explosion woke my husband and me out of a deep sleep. It sounded very near and very devastating. My husband bolted out of bed yelling, "Get the kids! Get the kids! They've bombed the city! We've got to get out of here!"

"Wait a minute," I said, grabbing him. "I think it was

thunder. Is it raining? Don't wake the kids yet. Turn on the television—or better yet, call the police department and see what they say."

He ran downstairs, turned on the TV, but didn't wait before calling the local police. I stood frozen in the dark hallway between our children's rooms, straining my ears for the sound of sirens or the reassuring rumble of simple thunder. Instead, I heard my husband hang up the phone, and by his slow, weary steps, I knew what he would report. He said that it was in fact thunder; the police told him that several other people had called thinking the same thing. *Thank God we didn't wake the kids,* I thought. Still, both of us were shaking as we lay silent in the darkness listening to the rain.

Two weeks later, I was sitting in my daughter's third-grade classroom at Back to School Night. Life was going on, but not exactly as usual. Everything was subdued and slightly surreal. Sixteen people had died in our small town of Rye, yet kids needed to go to school, people needed to go to work, and the routines of the living had to continue. Next to me that night was the mother of one of my daughter's classmates. As we began to talk, I said to her, "Wait a minute! Are you the bishop's wife?"

"Yes!" she told me with a smile. "And you must be the chaplain."

Earlier in the week, I had been helping out at a Girl Scout meeting when a little girl named Clara had informed me that her father was some sort of bishop. She was not nearly as impressed as I was. Apparently she and my daughter had been talking and made the discovery that both of them had clergy parents. Clara could not tell me what kind of bishop he was, or what denomination, but I was intrigued.

Now I found myself sitting next to her mother, the bishop's wife, Brook Packard. We laughed at how our daughters had found each other. Then our discussion quickly turned to the attacks on September 11. Brook told me that her husband, George, was the Episcopal bishop to the armed forces. He (and she) had gone to Ground Zero immediately after the attacks, and now George was directly involved in gathering clergy for service there. I told Brook about my background with hospice, with the dying and the dead, with grief and crisis intervention, and asked her to let the bishop know that I would be willing to help if needed. She seemed genuine when she thanked me, but she also informed me that he had been inundated with calls from clergy making the same offer. "But I'll let him know," Brook said, squeezing my hand.

About a week later, Bishop Packard called and said that he might need someone to fill a shift at Ground Zero. It was his shift, but he was scheduled to go to California that night. He wasn't promising anything, but he suggested we meet to talk about it. The only time he had was on Saturday morning while his daughter was playing soccer. We decided to look for each other at the game. It occurred to me as I headed onto the soccer fields that I had no idea what this man looked like. His daughter, like mine, played recreational soccer, which meant that there were at least half a dozen games going on at once, on small fields that blended together. There would be sidelines jammed with parents and brothers and sisters, with dogs and babysitters, and bigger children waiting their turn to play. There would be a line at the ice cream truck, and there would be no flashing sign over anybody's head saying, "September 11. September 11. Sign up here."

As I started across the field, however, I spotted him immediately. I later joked that he had that "holy air" about him, that bishop thing, but it really was the truth. He was walking about thirty yards ahead of me, hands behind his back, head inclined toward the ground. Even dressed in jeans and a casual shirt, moving in a sea of other parents, he was clearly the bishop. I had no doubt. When he lifted his eyes, I could see in them the weary wisdom of one who has endured much, and I felt in my own chest the resonance of a heart broken from bearing the weighty grief of others.

"George?" I said, as I approached him.

"Yes, hi." He smiled, slightly startled.

We stood and talked as the children played. I told him a little about myself, but I knew that the words were secondary to what he was seeking—a feeling, an impression. Could I be trusted with this task? Was I the right person to send in his place tonight? He said he would call if he needed me. I felt grateful just to have met him.

Around six o'clock that evening, the phone rang, and George asked if I could take his shift for the night—midnight to 8:00 AM. I said I would be honored. We made arrangements for him to stop by my house to give me instructions and identification. He told me over the phone to wear my collar and anything else that might identify me as clergy—a stole, a badge, anything. After some effort, I managed to dig up the clergy collar that I seldom wear. It's something I have never been very comfortable with. Perhaps it's because, where I come from in Ohio, Methodist ministers never wear them, or maybe I'm still not used to the curious stares I receive when I don it. In fact, one of the things I loved about being a hospice chaplain is that I had an excuse for not wearing the collar. I worked with people of all faiths, and I honored that by not dressing in something representative of one particular point of view.

What I soon came to realize, however, was how helpful the collar was at Ground Zero. There, it identified me; it set me apart from the civilian volunteers, from the Red Cross and the Salvation Army. It invited particular kinds of conversation; it offered comfort. It preceded me like a town crier, shouting, "In spite of what you see before you, God is here! God has not forgotten! God has the nerve to show up in all shapes and sizes and colors. Tonight God appears as a woman with long hair and a clergy collar. Go figure."

Bishop Packard knew that I would need everything I had to get me past the security checkpoints. The organization of pastoral care efforts at Ground Zero was still rather chaotic. The well-meaning and the simply curious were finding their way onto the site, some gawking, others proselytizing. Security was getting necessarily tighter, and therefore harder to penetrate, even for those who were authorized. I knew the other unspoken concern was the fact that I am a woman, and do not exactly look the part of a priest.

When the bishop arrived at my house, he offered me his field stole, his hard hat, and a paper mask. He also gave me an Episcopal chaplain's pin, an ID badge, the cell phone numbers of various priests who could help if I ran into trouble, instructions on where to go and how to get there, and he offered a prayer. I remember looking into his eyes as he was talking to me and thinking, *If this man trusts me with this task, then by the grace of God, I can do it.*

Before leaving, Bishop Packard enfolded my husband and me in an embrace. Our children were upstairs, and the three of us stood in the quiet of the living room with our arms around one another. I don't remember the words he said, but I remember the feeling of having been in the presence of a deep spirit, and this somehow comforted and strengthened me. With an "Amen," he slipped into the night. *I will pray for you, George Packard,* I remember thinking as I watched him leave. *I will pray for your safety and health because we need you on this planet.*

After putting the children to bed, my husband and I discussed whether I should take the train or drive to the area. Given the late hour, I decided to drive, which I never did again until late in the spring. I remember a long embrace before I left. "Call me when you get there, okay?" my husband said. His voice was full of concern and support. "And call if you need help with directions."

"I will!" I said, walking quickly to my car. "I love you."

In those early weeks, we could only drive so far south on the FDR Drive; the usual exits for the World Trade Center area were closed. I wasn't sure how close I could get when I set out, but I knew, eventually, I would have to ditch my car for the subway.

I called my husband twice on my way downtown for help

with exits, before finding a twenty-four-hour garage on Houston—then called him again when I emerged out of the subway station at Fulton and Broadway in front of St. Paul's Chapel. I didn't call him again until 8:30 the next morning, when I was nearly home.

10

WALKING THE SITE LIKE GOD

GETTING PAST THE BARRICADES proved easier than I had thought. Bishop Packard had prepared me well. Once into the restricted area, I headed immediately to St. Paul's Episcopal Chapel to report my arrival. From there, I was instructed to walk the site, to pay attention to the workers, to offer consolation and comfort, to be a presence and a support. I was not yet assigned to the morgue. That would come in November, when the Red Cross took over the organizing and scheduling of chaplains. This first night, I was on my own to go where I felt called, and to stay alert to those in need.

I left St. Paul's and walked toward what would be referred to forever as Ground Zero. My heart was pounding a little. I wasn't sure if it was fear or adrenaline. It was a cool, clear October night. The area was crowded with fire trucks from all over the tristate area. There were police and emergency medical personnel on every corner. The ragged remains of buildings rimmed the site like battered sentries. And in the middle of it all was a smoldering pile of wreckage. The size of it was absolutely staggering. I watched as men formed a human chain, handing bucketfuls of debris down the line. *How are they ever going to clear that pile using buckets?* I wondered. Still, they worked. They worked without ceasing.

In some ways, they were the lucky ones. At least they had something to do. For many others, there was a lot of standing around and waiting; and with the waiting came the speculating. Was it still possible to find someone alive? Maybe some people were in the subway tunnels. There were all kinds of snack shops down there, weren't there? Was it true some old man had ridden a piece of the building down several stories and survived? It's barely been three weeks since the attack. People have lived that long with almost nothing to eat, haven't they?

Talk floated on the brisk night air. As I passed by, I was usually greeted with a smile, a nod, or a friendly wave. About every ten yards, I would stop and talk to someone. Nearly everyone had a story. A fireman from a company in the Bronx told me about having been here on the eleventh. He told of the horrors of digging with his bare hands, of feeling something soft in the rocks and rubble and unearthing what turned out to be a woman's breast. Another told of discovering the intact body of a woman. As he moved toward her, her head turned. He explained how he stumbled backward, nearly jumping out of his skin. Thinking he was seeing things, he moved toward her again, and the same thing happened—her head moved. Then he realized that a steel pole had run through the back of her skull, and every time he moved forward, he stepped on the pole, causing her head to turn a little.

I listened to the stories. I memorized the faces telling them. I looked into people's eyes and invited them to give me their pain momentarily, to pour it into the bottomless bucket I was extending with my heart, to drain the images of their horror, just a little, by the telling.

I imagined myself like a funnel; I didn't accumulate or hold on to their pain—I just helped them release it. Each time a conversation seemed to reach its conclusion, I would put my hand on a shoulder or an arm, and promise to pray for the person I was talking with. And I did. I still do. I tried to lighten their burdens just a little; I tried to affirm them and support them. The collar that I had felt so ambivalent about wearing was actually an open invitation to talk. And I realized that I was grateful for it. I couldn't fathom at the time how important it was for workers to see a clergy presence at Ground Zero; but a year or so later, I read someone describe us this way: "They walked the site like God." Clearly, in times of crisis, it is essential to bear witness to the fact that we are not alone in the world. Even through the darkest valleys, we are not forsaken. And no one is forgotten.

There were also glimmers of grace on this first night, and these moments made me smile. For instance, as I made my way along a particularly desolate block, a couple of young police officers approached me anxiously. "Hey, Reverend, Reverend!" they called. "You are a reverend, aren't you?"

"Yes," I said. There was an urgency in their voices that made me think they were going to direct me to someone in need. My first impulse was that *they* were okay but were worried about someone else. I was half right—but not in the way that I had anticipated.

"Listen, we were just wondering what the difference is between a Catholic and a Protestant."

When I heard this, I felt my whole body exhale and my heart lift. No longer on red alert, I could feel the cool wind in my hair, and the evening air coloring my cheeks. I was startled and refreshed because it seemed so random and sweet a question, so ordinary and out of context in this night of sadness and despair.

"You see," said one of the officers, "my buddy here is engaged to a Protestant and he's Catholic, and they were wondering how to bring up the kids. What do you think?"

I looked at them and smiled. Their faces were so animated and full of confidence. I knew they weren't asking me for a thesis on the Protestant Reformation. They didn't want to know my thoughts on Vatican II. They were looking, in their own way, for some kind of blessing and reassurance.

"Well," I started, "there's not much difference, really, when it comes to belief. They are both Christian religions. Catholics put more emphasis on the saints, on the veneration of Mary, and on the importance of the Pope. Protestants severed their connection to Rome and pretty much did away with confession. But the main difference is in how they are organized and who gets to be ordained. Obviously, I am a prime example. I could not be a Catholic priest—and neither could you if you were married."

"Thank God for that!" they laughed. "But what do you

think we should do?" asked the young officer, eyes open wide, trusting, expectant.

"I think you should decide who is most likely to take the kids to church. To whom is religion most important—you or your fiancée? Teach the children about both traditions, but bring them up in the faith of the most actively involved parent, because it really doesn't matter to God. Just love them, love each other, and do your best."

"You sure?" asked the future groom. "Both religions believe in Jesus and God and all that stuff?"

"Yup. I'm sure. I promise."

For a moment, we stood together like a sturdy three-legged stool under the starless sky. I am sure that we were encircled in light. And the light was called hope.

"Thanks, Rev!" they said after shaking my hand. I watched them walk away, still engaged in their discussion, hands gesturing, long legs moving in easy synchronicity. A flood of gratitude washed over me as I stood there. Thank God there are those who still hope, who still plan, who still have the gumption to get engaged and to marry and to worry about raising children who are not yet born. Thank God for those who still believe in the future. "Keep them safe," I whispered, sending a prayer flying toward their backs, like a mother running with hats that her boys forgot to put on. Then they disappeared around a corner as if exiting a stage. And the night and I resumed our quiet watch.

11

SAVING ANTHONY

ABOUT 3:30 IN THE morning, I approach the corner across from what is left of Building Five. Three police officers are stationed there. They are sitting on folding chairs, looking tired, frustrated, and a little bored. "Hey, Reverend," one of them calls as I come near, "we have an officer here who is in dire need of forgiveness. He's an atheist. What do you think we should do with him?" Reaching the officer in question, I offer a mock kick to his shins, which makes them laugh. It seems to take them by surprise; it also prompts them to welcome me into their company. Another chair is somehow found and offered to me. As I gratefully accept it, I realize that this is the first time I have sat down since arriving just before midnight.

"How're you guys holding up?" I ask.

"Beautiful, just beautiful," says one of the men with a smile. It seems to be an inside joke, because they all laugh. I have the feeling they say this because there is no real way of answering that question. How *could* they be feeling, after all? What can they say, how can they put into words the effect of guarding this post? They are participants in the investigation of a crime for which there is no precedent. And so, if laughter escapes, it is heavy and tinged with melancholy.

Our conversation starts like a dance between strangers, a bit tentative and shy, until the rhythm of the stories begins to carry us. Soon the men are openly sharing their disbelief and horror over this terrible event. Though the evidence of it is right before our eyes, it is nearly impossible to take in. "I still can't believe it," confesses one of the officers, shaking his head. "I'm down here every night on this same corner, looking at the same mess, and I still can't believe it's real." Along with disbelief, there is palpable frustration. All had hoped that survivors would be pulled from the rubble. All had hoped that there would be something more for them to do than stand guard over what is feeling more and more like a graveyard. These men are trained to save lives, to stop crimes, to enforce some decent rule of law. None of them could have fathomed that one day they would be guarding the ghostly remains of part of the city they loved and nearly three thousand of her people. The night passes slowly for those whose only task is to watch and wait.

The men talk of the stress on their families. They talk of their first glimpses of violence as young cops, and of the images that never seem to leave them. They ask me about myself, about my work, and how I have come to be there with them. They listen attentively as I speak. The conversation now has an easy, gentle flow. Were it not for the grim backdrop of Ground Zero, one might mistake it for small talk. But upon closer observation, the sadness and fatigue which tug at the corners of their eyes, and the yearning they have to tell their stories, and the images they share bear witness to heartbreak and trauma. These men will never be the same.

When our conversation seems to reach its natural conclusion, this particular dance over, I decide to continue on my rounds. They smile and say to stop back if I have the chance. I get the feeling that they are reluctant to let me go. The time we spent together, however brief, has provided a welcome relief from the oppressive monotony and frustration of their shifts. To tell the truth, it is a little hard for me to move on, too, because I know that I will have to start all over again with the next person or group of people I encounter. But it is time; so I take a deep breath, say thanks for the chair, and go on my way.

For a few moments, I stand alone, looking at the pile of debris and the surrounding wreckage. I clear my mind so that I can make room for more stories, more pain. I tuck them away carefully, not to be suppressed but to be preserved. When I can feel my spirit lifting, my mind clearing, the scene around me comes into sharp focus. Perhaps the stories I have heard have released the voices and faces of the human beings buried there . . . perhaps the stories have unblocked my ears and my heart. I stand without moving, breathing slowly and deeply, as if in meditation, opening myself, and allowing the Spirit to break through.

I'm not sure how many minutes go by, but soon I become

aware of a groan emanating from the pile. It is as if someone has slowly turned up the volume from an invisible speaker. Some might say that this is my imagination. No matter. How can anyone explain a spiritual experience without sounding slightly mad? Smoke is rising into the black night air—and permeating it all is the swirling, unseen presence of the dead. I am sure that it is palpable and audible for anyone who dares to feel or to listen. My impression is that some of the dead are moaning in anguished confusion, trying to figure out what has happened to them, while others cry out because they know. I also intuit the presence of other, higher spiritual beings trying to guide them gently away from the scene of their deaths.

"Go," I whisper into the night. "Don't stay here. You are free now. This has nothing to do with you. We will look for your bodies. We will honor you. But go. Be at peace."

In the months to follow, I will experience the gradual diminishing of these groans. "Perhaps I just got used to being on-site," I will say when asked. But deep down, I will always believe that I heard them, and that eventually all who were suffering did in fact find their way home.

I begin walking again, turning my attention to the living—but the dead and I have become permanently acquainted. They walk with me as I circle the site, guiding me to those in need. They accompany me as I make my way past tattered buildings that will soon come down, past construction trucks and fire trucks, past men in hard hats and uniforms. And they will eventually give me the strength to see their broken bodies and to offer blessing.

For an hour or two, I weave a path among the countless

men and women who are working, perhaps unknowingly, in the company of the dead. Immersed in thought, I am startled to find myself passing the same corner occupied by the officers who had offered me the chair. They wave me over like they have something important to discuss, something they have been thinking about since I left them.

"Hey, guys, what's up?" I ask.

The captain tells me about an officer in his precinct. At first, I think he is just teasing me, having a little fun at my expense—but the more he talks, the more genuine seems his concern.

"I've got this guy, Anthony," he begins. "And believe you me, Reverend, he needs saving. This guy is such a bad apple. He cheats on his wife, he runs around constantly with other women . . . It's bad for morale at the station. I mean, we can't take it anymore. You've got to save him, Rev, put the fear of God back into him."

I look at the captain, studying his face, and then at the other two officers. This wasn't at all what I had expected, but it seems to be what God is presenting me with. "What do you suggest?" I ask. "Do you want me to offer him some sort of opportunity for confession? Do you want me to help you confront him? Or do you just want me to tell him that God has told me everything he's been doing and he'd better stop?"

I am joking about the latter, of course, but the captain and his companions begin to hatch a plan to save their fellow officer. I am fully aware that this is born most likely out of a desire to break the unbearable heaviness and monotony of their night, and to distract them, even momentarily, from the senseless destruction in which they are entrenched. I wonder again how concerned they actually are for Anthony's soul.

"This is what you do," says the captain with a twinkle in his eye. "See that guy on the corner? That's Anthony's partner. Ask for Anthony. Say he helped you out once and you want to say thank you."

"Where's Anthony?" I ask, beginning to get a queasy feeling in my stomach.

"He's asleep in the police van there."

"Wait a minute! You want me to wake up an officer who's been working all night just to pull a prank on him?"

"First of all, he's been sleeping too long. Second of all, Rev, this is not a prank. It's for his own good, remember? This is for his soul and for the morale of the precinct. He won't know if you're someone he met at a bar or what—and I guarantee he'll start hitting on you."

"Come on, guys, I'm too old for this," I argue, suddenly feeling a little ridiculous and wishing I were still the twenty-six-year-old I was when I was first ordained.

"Please, Reverend. Please do this for us," they plead. "We've been down here every night since this thing happened, and, trust us, there are not too many opportunities for a little levity. Besides, his behavior really is detrimental to the other guys in the precinct."

I look into the blue, bloodshot eyes of the captain and then to his fellow officers; I look from one to the other to the other. Sighing, I put my head in my hands and reluctantly say, "Okay. Okay. I will do this for you. I will do this for Anthony and for you, his comrades." *Is this professional?* I ask myself. *Is it appropriate? Is it disrespectful? Would the bishop approve?* I don't have time to ponder these questions; the wheels have already started moving. I take a deep breath and head with long, determined strides for the corner where Anthony's partner is sitting. Instinctively, I pull out the white tab from my clergy collar and tuck it into my pocket. I give my hair a shake and square my shoulders. "God, forgive me," I mutter, glancing up at the not yet dawning sky.

As I near the corner, I glance over my shoulder and can see the creeping shadows of the officers, who have followed me. They are hiding behind trailers and vans to get a good view of their wayward colleague about to be busted by the female priest. It is too late to turn back, so I ignore my ambivalence and my reservations, and ask for Anthony. His partner jumps up a little too quickly, like he's accustomed to strange women asking for his friend. Despite my fake protests, the partner says he'll go and wake Anthony from the trailer.

After a minute or two, Anthony emerges, sleepy-eyed but smoothing his hair. No, he's not sure he remembers me. How long has it been? I bluff. I smile. I say it's okay if he doesn't remember. Meanwhile, I can see that the half-hidden officers are enjoying this. They are beginning to stifle silent laughter in the shadows; I can see their shoulders shaking. As if on cue, Anthony begins to work his charm. When do I finish my shift? Will I be coming down regularly to help out? True to his reputation, but obviously not to his wedding vows, Officer Anthony makes his move: Do I have a number where he can reach me?

No longer able to contain themselves, the captain and his

fellow officers jump out of hiding and begin to verbally accost him.

"Anthony, do you know who this is? This is a priest you're trying to pick up! That's practically like hitting on God! You're going straight to hell, Anthony. Do you hear me?" says the captain with a triumphant laugh. *Straight . . . to . . . hell!*"

Anthony tries to protest as he looks at me in disbelief. He says he wasn't really trying to hit on me, but no one is buying it. With each denial, the other officers get more animated. Not to be outdone, Anthony turns to me and says with a smile, "So, what time *do* you get off?" The officers laugh, as we turn to walk away. But their laughter dies quickly, like a match in the wind, as we head toward our posts.

"Thanks, Rev," the captain says softly as heaviness begins to creep into his eyes again. "You really made our night. Thanks a lot for being here. For all of us."

"I'll keep Anthony in my prayers," I say, shaking his hand. "And you, too. Be careful, okay?"

"Hey, we're always careful, right, fellas?"

"Sure," one of them answers. "Beautiful."

12

THE MORGUE CALLS

A s morning dawned, my shift came to an end. I watched the sky change from purple to pink to blue, watercolors running and seeping across a giant canvas. Workers were steadily coming and going, the ready replacing the weary. They nodded to one another, they shook hands, they filled one another's shoes. The site, too, seemed to shift and change. The ghosts were quiet. Maybe they were observing us, maybe they were sleeping; or maybe they were just drowned out by the bustle of a new day, camouflaged by the light. I went into St. Paul's to say good-bye and to let the priest in charge know that I was leaving. Then I boarded the subway, got off several blocks uptown, found my car, and started the drive home.

The FDR was humming with morning commuters. Luckily for me, most of them were heading south. The northbound side, on which I was traveling, was smooth and fast. Cars wove in and out of the lanes like sewing needles stitching a pattern.

As for me, I just drove. I could not process. I could not think profound thoughts or even, momentarily, recall some of my conversations. Each mile brought me closer to my life, closer to the ordinary realities that filled my days—my family, my job, the responsibilities of living. And yet something had shifted in me. It was imperceptible, really—but I knew that I had made a heart commitment to the workers and the victims at Ground Zero.

I arrived home just in time to kiss my children as they left for school. "Are you okay, Mommy?" my daughter asked, wide-eyed. "I'm so glad you're home."

"I'm fine, honey," I said as I gave her an extralong squeeze. "I'm fine."

I rested for two hours before heading to my job at hospice. There were patients to see, families to help. Death loomed like a shadow. I could not help but make the comparison between having the opportunity to prepare for death and dying suddenly, between gently assisting a family through the dying process and looking for the shattered remains of loved ones who just never came home from work. Grief is grief, as some would say, but it does matter how one dies and how remains are handled. It matters to those who are still here, those who must come to terms with living without a loved one.

I completed my day vaguely aware of the lack of support I felt from my colleagues. Most knew why I was late to work, yet only one or two people asked me how I was. I observed their silence as if from a distance. The concern was not that I had stayed up all night helping those working downtown but whether I could be present to our patients. I admired their commitment to maintaining excellent care, and the unspoken reminder that these patients were important, but I found it disheartening that so few coworkers could find it in themselves to ask, "How ya doin'?"

This continued to be the case throughout my months of service downtown. There were exceptions, but I still find it curious and infuriating when I reflect back on that time. My commitment to hospice never wavered, nor did I ever underestimate the pain of these families; but, for a time, I had to stretch. Sometimes I was tired. Sometimes, I'm sure, I was numb. But always I tried to give the best I had, aware that this acute crisis in our nation's history would pass, even if its impact on me would remain.

A few weeks went by. Then, on November 13, 2001, I found myself in a room at the offices of the Episcopal Diocese of New York with about fifty other ministers, priests, and rabbis. The Rev. Tom Faulkner, an Episcopal priest, had called us together on behalf of the Red Cross, who were now officially taking over the organizing of chaplains at Ground Zero. No one was sure what this change of leadership would mean, but Tom assured everyone that it would help smooth our efforts.

The atmosphere was both determined and anxious. It was the day after Flight 587 had crashed in Queens. The plane had been headed to Santo Domingo in the Dominican Republic but fell from the sky shortly after takeoff, killing all 260 people onboard and 5 on the ground. Though terrorism was ruled out fairly quickly, it was obviously on all of our minds. An announcement was made that there was still a need for clergy at the airport, where families were gathering, as well as at the crash site to offer blessings over the dead and support to the workers. Anyone who was able to volunteer for this effort was directed to gather immediately after our meeting.

I considered whether it would be possible for me to volunteer. The impulse to offer my services was tempered by the reality that I needed coverage for my children. This would be a frequent dilemma for me as I volunteered at Ground Zero: how to balance my call to service with my commitment to family. I envied those whose children were grown, or who had no family responsibilities. As much as I felt I could be helpful, I knew that this time I would have to pass.

During the meeting, the various opportunities for ministry at Ground Zero were outlined. There would be several family centers, St. Paul's Chapel, the Marriott Hotel (where meals were currently being offered to workers), the Permanent Morgue, which was off-site, and the Temporary Morgue located at Ground Zero. I knew, without hesitation, that my call was to the Temporary Morgue, or the T-Mort, as it came to be known. I felt that my experience with the dying and the dead had prepared me as well as it could for being on hand to offer blessings over remains and comfort to the bereaved. I could not truly fathom what awaited me, or any of us, at the T-Mort. We were simply moving with whatever current was carrying us to our places of service. For me, volunteering at the morgue was the only choice. In a strange way, I knew that I would be most at home there—at home with the dead and with the people who were working so hard to honor them.

Ministry at the morgue did not entail therapy, and it did not involve religious service in a traditional way. As the days unfolded, our mission became clear. We were to offer a quiet ministry of presence at a time of utter despair. We were to walk with the weary and the broken, to offer blessings over the remains of colleagues and strangers, to lift the human spirit if possible, and to bear witness to the enduring Beauty of life. Anyone who served at Ground Zero, who walked with fellow workers through that valley of the shadow of death, encountered terrible destruction and unbearable sorrow. But what we left with, miraculously, was a pearl of great price: the awareness of the Holy, living and vibrant, in the eyes of other human beings.

13

MIST AND VAPOR

Y ou might want a little of this," says the cop standing next to me, holding a jar of mentholated vapor rub. He swipes some around his nostrils, getting a little in his mustache, and offers some to me. As I meet his eyes, he says, "It doesn't help much, but it's something. This one's gonna be bad." I hesitate but do as he suggests, rubbing the base of my nose with the ointment. The menthol clears my sinuses with its cool, sharp vapor. It reminds me of being a child, when my mother would rub my chest with Vicks. I remember her silhouette appearing against the light in the hall as she entered my dark, little room. The sweetness of her voice and her gentle touch almost made it worth being sick. I would surrender to the sound of her, the feel of her, trusting implicitly in her care for me. As she disappeared back into the light, I would snuggle down into the soft darkness of my room, breathe in the familiar vapor, and know that everything would be better in the morning.

But now I am standing in the harsh glare of a fluorescent light. And what emerges from the doorway beyond our trailer is not my mother with her healing touch but a large black body bag. Everything has been turned inside out. The darkness is not cozy—it is terrifying. It holds the gruesome reality of our worst nightmares. It lurks behind curtains of concrete and mud, steel and shattered glass. And the light? The light, too, has lost its comfort. It is no longer where mothers appear and disappear to keep the world in order; it is where we are forced to bear witness time and again to the unthinkable.

The body bag is placed on one of the receiving tables. It is obvious that it contains a sizable human remain. I feel my chest tighten and my breath constrict. *Oh, dear God,* I say to myself, *please help me.* But nothing can prepare us for this ritual. No matter how many bags are brought in, no matter how many bodies or fragments of bodies we see, the shock of opening that bag is always the same. Dear God dear God dear God. How many times can the heart be broken? *Just once more,* you always think to yourself. *I can do it one more time. We can do it. Steady now. Pass me the Vicks, brother. Pass me the Vicks.*

We assemble, as always, in silence. The bag is unzipped. Holy God. There is the torso of a man in what looks to have been a white, button-down shirt. There is no head. There is nothing beyond the tops of the hips. The shirt is shredded and muddy. The rib cage exposed. There are no arms or hands. God have mercy. The Vicks doesn't really help. This one has been imprisoned for too long below the rubble. Decay is in my mouth. It is in my throat. It is in my soul now, too. As I inhale, the dead lodge themselves within me. I will carry them around in my body, in my gut, in my mucous membranes, and in my cells. This one is stuck in my chest. *Someone's father,* I keep thinking. *Someone's son.* We go about our work like phantoms, like holograms of ourselves. No one looks away. We cannot look away. *Bear witness,* this torso of a man whispers. *This happened. I died. Live anyway. Keep breathing.*

The blessing is the last thing that happens before the bag is zipped closed. I am aware that my words will fall like mist, like dew, like an anointing or baptism. I will rub this chest with the vapor of my breath, with words, because that is all I have. Will they soothe? Will they comfort? Will they be enough?

Without knowing it, we form a circle of light around the man—but it is not the harsh glare of fluorescent light. It is the warm glow from the hallway, from childhoods where life made sense, and mothers came when you were afraid, and darkness was only a blanket you snuggled into on your way to a delicious dream. We do the best we can in our too bright trailer. With our presence and our words and our broken hearts, we rock this man on his makeshift bed, tuck him in, then send him gently on his way toward home. *Now perhaps he can rest,* I think. But for those of us who remain, it is more complicated. We stand, dumbfounded, blinking in the light, like those waving from a train platform. He is gone, but we are here, waiting for the darkness to surrender, once again, that which it has stolen.

14

ADAM'S HAND

IT IS A RAINY November afternoon at the site. I have been in the morgue for a couple of hours talking to the EMTs and cops, but it has been quiet in terms of remains. All of us hope the phone will ring or a radio will announce a new discovery. In the meantime, we make ourselves busy. We talk, we stretch; we stare at the ceiling. We decide to get a bite at St. Paul's or the Marriott or the Salvation Army Respite Center, fondly referred to as the big bubble. I am free to walk the site, to stop and talk to workers, and to pause for a while with those who need to tell their stories.

I step out into the drizzle, put my head down, and walk to the corner closest to where the south tower stood. The world is monochromatic; everything melts together in a watery gray—the sky, the muddy ground, the buildings. Trucks and machinery drone on without ceasing, providing a perfect sound track for the dreariness of the day. The air smells of diesel and muck and who knows what else. It has a bitter and peculiar taste, and burns my eyes and throat. It crosses my mind that we are all swimming in a toxic cesspool, but what can we do?

"It's bad down here today," says a police officer on the corner without much expression. I nod in agreement and shudder a little. As we begin to make small talk, I notice the familiar resignation that has wrapped itself around him. I have the feeling that he, like so many others, has been here too often, has seen too much, and that no amount of rest can ease his weariness now. It has settled in his bones, in his identity. We slip into an easy exchange about everyday life. The officer is in his early forties. "If I could retire tomorrow, I would," he tells me. "I could practically retire now, but it just doesn't seem like the right time to leave. It would feel unpatriotic, you know? I couldn't leave now." We talk of his children. Yes, they are proud of him. Yes, they worry. Yes, there is a strain on his marriage with all the time he is putting in at the Trade Center.

"I've gone to too many funerals and memorials," he tells me. "At the last one I went to, a twelve-year-old girl gave the eulogy for her dad. She was the same age as my daughter. All I could think of was that no kid should have to do that. No kid should lose her father this way. Right then and there, I decided to get out when I can so that my daughters won't have to do that for me."

"You're a young man," I say. "What kind of work do you think you will do after you leave the police force?"

"I don't know, but it'll have nothing to do with law enforcement. Maybe something like landscaping. Be outside. Make something grow."

I put my hand on his arm for a moment and look into his face. There is still something alive there—a shimmer of color amidst all this grayness, like a green shoot pushing its way through a crack in the cement.

"Do that," I say to him. "In the meantime, teach your girls."

"Thanks," he says, with a faint smile. "Take care."

With that he dismisses me. One can only talk so much here. I understand, and I keep moving.

November becomes December, and the days begin to blur. I now have trouble remembering what I did on a particular shift. With whom did I talk? What part of someone did I bless? Between volunteering at the morgue, working at hospice, and taking care of my children, I am beginning to forget—or am I storing the memories away in some locked vault of me? I feel as shattered as the skull fragment before me. It is night again, and I find myself looking blankly at the smooth bone which the medical examiner turns over in his hand like a small stone. I imagine that he is going to skip it across some placid lake, like I used to do with rocks when I was young. I no longer bother with the mentholated ointment. I know too well that nothing can blot out the reality of death that permeates our lives here.

Once identified, the skull fragment is gently set aside. There is tissue. There are random, unidentifiable bone chips. Then the medical examiner carefully extracts what turns out to be a left hand from the bag on the table. Someone lets out a soft, anguished groan. The sound escapes not because of the grimness of the discovery but because of what hangs precariously on the tip of one finger—a wedding ring. It is a miracle which we all recognize immediately. How they managed to extract this hand from that hellish mess with the ring still there seems impossible. The ring circles the last knuckle of the ring finger, which is curled ever so slightly toward the palm—just enough to have kept its treasure. Kept its promise. The hand is blackened and somewhat atrophied. And yet it is beautiful. A man's hand bearing witness to love. A man's hand bearing witness to the excruciating care of those who unearthed it. A man's hand which was once a boy's, which was formed in his mother's womb, which first was feather soft as it curled in a tiny fist, which grew to hold a ball, to roll a truck, to move a pencil, to write a name. This hand waved hello to friends; it tied shoes and buttoned shirts. This hand tenderly caressed a spouse; it was offered to another in love as a life together began. Did it also hold a child's hand? Did it rock a cradle, hold a bottle? Did it fix a broken toy? Someone will get their husband's ring back, we whisper. Unbelievable.

It rests before us now, as if plucked from the ceiling of the Sistine Chapel. As such, it is more than the hand of this particular man—it is the hand of a saint. It is Michelangelo's Adam reaching for God, or God reaching for us. It is the charred evidence of when life leapt like a spark from the Divine. We cannot speak. This hand reaches for us in all its aching beauty as if to say, "Behold. Behold the utter stupidity and brutality of the human race. Behold its stubborn grace. I made you. I reached for you, and once you knew enough to reach for me. I encircled you in love. I cling to you still, like this golden circle. Reach for me again, and live."

Two years later, I will dream that I am carrying this hand, now restored to a healthy, fleshy pink. It is my job to find to whom it belongs. I am walking quickly down unfamiliar streets, looking, looking, looking for the owner. I know that he is here somewhere. I am sorry that it has taken me so long. I am determined but bewildered. I continue searching as I cradle it in my own two hands. "Where are you? Where are you?" I call.

But before this night is even thinking about becoming a dream, I return home exhausted, drop my clothes on the floor, and curl into bed. It is nearly 2:00 AM. "Are you okay?" my husband asks sleepily. "They found a hand with a wedding ring," I whisper. And then I begin to cry.

15

FLAGS AND TAGS

Another Saturday night at the morgue. A body bag lies on one of the stainless steel tables. It is not one of the small red bundles that are often lying there, usually containing but a fragment of human remains. This one contains the nearly intact body of a construction worker. A teamster, I'm told. The blessing has already been given by the chaplain preceding me. I just missed him. Subway seemed to take forever from Grand Central tonight.

I check in at the Temporary Morgue, introducing myself to the captain in charge and leaving my cell phone number on the wall. Then I meet my husband and two children on the sidewalk in the nonrestricted area. For the first time since I began volunteering at the morgue, they have ridden the train down with me. I wanted them to get a glimpse of where I go. Take some of the anxiety out of it for the children. As we begin the walk down to St. Paul's, they seem to respond to the pulse of life in the cold January air. The sidewalks are crowded with people. The night smells of pretzels and roasted nuts, of hot dogs and, occasionally, wet concrete. As we approach St. Paul's, I see that there is a long line of people waiting to walk out onto the new viewing platform. They need to see, we all need to see; it is our communal tragedy. But I know that, no matter how long they look, it will never make sense. The only thing that makes sense is their presence. Someone needs to bear witness to what is happening here every hour, every minute of every long day and lonely night.

We duck into the church. It envelops us in its hushed peace, offering a welcome contrast to the bustle outside. A violin and a piano play a soft, haunting tune. Cops and firemen are scattered throughout the pews. Some sit alone, staring straight ahead; some talk quietly to one another. Food and coffee are offered and gratefully accepted. There is an awkward line for a bathroom that was never intended to accommodate such a volume of patrons. A young man in uniform appears almost unconscious as he stretches out on a massage therapist's table. I envy her ability to offer something of concrete comfort to these men and women. By now, I am well acquainted with their stories of standing for hours in the bitter cold. *Rest,* I think to myself, looking at him. *Rest and surrender to a moment of peace.*

I sit with my family for a while in one of the pews. There are pillows scattered throughout the benches. The church walls are covered with notes, banners, cards, and pictures from all over the world. They offer support, encouragement, gratitude, and comfort. *Holy graffiti,* I think to myself. *Holy graffiti.*

Soon I feel the morgue tugging at me. My phone hasn't rung, but I feel anxious to get going. We emerge from the church and head back toward the Temporary Morgue. I say good-bye to my husband and children on the street. My daughter keeps turning around to wave. Her face is filled with a mixture of awe and anxiety. *What is she thinking?* I wonder. *What can she comprehend? What fears and images creep into her eight-year-old head?* My son skips beside my husband, eyes drinking in all the men in uniform. Living G.I. Joes. He is spared the enormity of the event because he is six years old and life is still magical and sane.

I open the door to the morgue and see a couple of EMTs I've met here before. I'm amazed at how good it is to see a familiar face, to feel a sense of continuity, to skip the introductions and the work it takes to establish a rapport. Most of my contacts here, most of those with whom I have had conversations, I never see again. We meet, I hear their stories, our hearts connect, then—gone. Their faces will fade before their stories, I suppose.

It soon gets busy. A couple of bags of remains are brought in. At this point, the magic number is three. When three bags are brought in, the medical examiner and crime scene investigator will be called, and the procedure in the morgue will begin. This procedure differs only if a full body or the remains of a man or woman of service is brought in. Then there is no waiting.

Two bundles in red plastic bags sit on the receiving table. A TV is perched precariously on top of a tall, metal shelf. CNN is broadcasting the news of a small plane that has crashed into a building in Tampa. I feel numb as I watch the story unfold. A weary-looking EMT says, to no one in particular, "I bet it was a suicide. That's just my feeling. Feels like a suicide." The next day, I hear on the news that he is right. The fifteen-year-old student pilot left a note saying that he endorsed the terrorism of September 11. But tonight, we can only speculate (if we have the interest or the energy to do so). Conversation drifts. Workers come and go. There is a shift change. Badges and radios and keys are exchanged.

The EMS lieutenant in charge begins to tell me of his youngest daughter, who has a history of running away from home. She suffers from bipolar disorder, he says. Out of the blue, he informs me that he oscillates between being a heathen and being an agnostic. I'm not sure how he would define these, but it doesn't matter. "I believe in God," he says, "but who's to say that Islam is not the way?" I smile, knowing that he is not looking for an answer—he is nudging me, sticking his toe into the water to see how I will react. I ask him more about his family. He takes a Christmas cookie out of a box next to him and pops it into his mouth. "Look at me," he says. "Eating cookies in the morgue. Pretty gross, eh?" "That's what they're there for," I answer. But I, too, am aware of the remains on the table next to me. Whenever someone walks past, the smell of decay catches in my throat.

How strangely comfortable we have become with the bits of humanity waiting patiently in their bags. Patience has become a necessary part of survival here. To watch the pieces of people being extracted from that pit is to watch something of extraordinary patience and commitment. Much of the work is done by hand. When it was clear that no life would be pulled from the wreckage, the meticulous collecting of remains began. It is holy work. And what is most miraculous of all is the fact that everyone senses this. When conversation goes on in the morgue, with people seemingly oblivious to the fact that there is some bit of someone sitting in that bag, it can be deceiving. No one has forgotten, not even for an instant. No one is unaware. No one is callous. They have only accepted, out of necessity, the pace of this process. For everyone here knows, when the bags are opened, they will not look away. There will be reverence and respect. A hush will fill the room. The medical examiner will gently and attentively struggle to make out what bit of the body is before him. The crime scene investigator will photograph the remains and document where the victim was found. An entry will be made into the log. A chaplain will offer a blessing. Grown men and women will cross themselves and bow their heads. And then it will be back to waiting and hoping that more remains will be recovered during the night, plucked from the dust and the anonymity of this communal grave.

Midway through the evening, one of the EMTs says that he is in need of more flags with which to drape the remains of the dead. Flags had originally been reserved for people of service but now are draped over any substantial body that is recovered. It is the right thing to do; for all who died were inadvertently drafted into service—for their country, for their coworkers, for the rest of us who remain, the walking wounded. The EMT tells us that some flags have been stolen off of his gator as he's driven through the streets. "Someone wanted to trade me a picture of the Trade Center for a flag," he says, shaking his head. There is not much response from the others in the morgue. A few people shrug and look idly away. The lieutenant says that he will get more flags right away.

About 11:00 PM, the lieutenant returns with two boxes of flags. As he lifts a box up to the top of a shelf, I can't help noticing that it goes right next to a box labeled TOE TAGS. *Flags and tags,* I say to myself. *This is what it has come down to, flags and tags.* The only problem is there are too few toes to tag. Most still lie hidden somewhere beneath the rubble or have been blown out to sea on the fall breeze, now turned cold. If we could find the dead, we would honor them. But for now, we can only be patient and wait.

16

STATION 10–10

IT IS GETTING CLOSE to midnight. I have had too much coffee, too many bottles of water, and have made too many trips to St. Paul's to use the bathroom. I decide to walk down to the fire station that sits on the edge of Ground Zero. Once nestled in the shadow of the mighty towers, it is a place that some workers avoid and others seek out like a holy shrine. The firefighters from this company were the first to respond when the planes hit. "All rushed in to help," I hear over and over. "No one came out." Someone tells me that all of the men from this station were killed on that morning because they were in the middle of a shift change. As the months pass, I learn that five men from Station 10–10 were killed that day—five more than anyone can bear—but not *all* of the men from this company. Truth and mythology mingle freely in the air in these early days of the recovery, adding to the haunting sense of tragedy and shock. For the moment, for those who walk the site, however, facts are less important than feelings, numbers less compelling than the battered station that still stands defiantly at its post.

Now the firehouse is ghostly quiet, save for a few scattered workers. Supplies have been organized in the bay that once housed a fire truck. Someone is on hand to give out gloves, hats, boots, socks, et cetera to the workers. As the hours pass, the man on duty sits at a makeshift desk talking quietly to those who come in and out. There are a variety of fire department patches scattered across the desk, free to whoever wants one. Another man sits behind a computer in a small office. He is in charge of satellite locating—when remains are found, he precisely charts the place, the position, and the time.

I offer the usual "How ya doin'?" to those men I pass. There *are* women here, but it is predominately a man's world at Ground Zero. When I worked my first shift, back in October, the air was positively humming with male energy, with testosterone, and with what could have been mistaken for bravado. But it was not bravado; it was the desperation of strong and able men who could not fathom that there was nothing they could do to save a life. They lined their trucks along the site, made plans, climbed the pile, passed buckets of debris like thimblefuls of ocean. They persisted with their broad shoulders and bare hands, with images of their children at home and their brothers underground, and they hoped.

Now, some four months later, they work continuously to find the bodies of those who eluded their best intentions to save. It requires tremendous strength and gut-wrenching commitment. But what always makes my throat tighten and my eyes well is the quiet tenderness with which they go about their work. "See how the driver of that bulldozer gives his bucket a little shake?" says a man standing next to me. "You know why he does that? He does that to make sure he doesn't have a piece of someone caught in his bucket. He's trying to see if anything can be shaken loose from the rubble so that no remains are lost." These men no longer hope for the rescue of victims, or even for whole bodies. Perhaps the only thing they hope is that no one will get hurt this night, or that sleep will come quickly when they finally go home.

As I step into Station 10–10, I give a small wave to the man tending the supplies and walk quietly into what was the dining room for those who belonged to this firehouse. It is as if the room has been frozen in time. No one uses this space out of respect for the men who died. Notes of upcoming events, long since past, hang on a wall. There are a few boxes of pancake mix and pasta on the counter. Pictures and plaques keep watch from their places as if standing guard. There is a feeling of warmth and familiarity, of comfort and casual ease. *They are never coming back,* I think. *They are never going to sit around this table and laugh at someone's stupid joke or argue over the Yankees and the Mets, the Jets and the Giants. No one will announce his engagement or the birth of a new baby.* "God bless you all," I whisper to no one—or to everyone.

I walk down the hall to use the bathroom. After shutting and locking the outside door, I am certain that I hear someone using the urinal next to my stall. My heart jumps. I look under the door but see no feet. With blood beginning to pump in my ears, I quickly finish and open the stall door. I notice that the water in the sink is running. *Was it running when I came in?* I wonder. Then I hear something behind me that sounds very much like someone ripping a paper towel out of the dispenser. No one there. My heart is now pounding. I open the door to the bathroom and nearly trip over a fireman who is on his hands and knees pulling duct tape off the carpet just outside the door. "Sorry," I say awkwardly, turning red. He looks up and smiles. His eyes are kind, his voice genuinely warm. "That's okay. Be careful now."

I feel a little ridiculous as I walk back through the doors into the night, but a lingering feeling of the unseen presence of those who died remains. A band of men who loved this house, who laughed and slept here, and did their jobs, are dead. *Are you here now?* I ask silently, looking up into the black night sky. *Are your bodies still out there? Are you okay? Are you trying to help?*

The slap of bitter cold January air interrupts my communion with the dead, and I walk with long, quick strides toward the morgue. I check my cell phone on the way. No calls. I feel as if I have been gone for hours, but it has been more like thirty minutes. Once inside the morgue trailer, which could never be described as cozy, I am comforted by the reality of live workers, with real voices and jobs to be done. As I slip into one of the folding chairs that line the wall, a female EMT asks me where I've been. "I went down to 10–10 to use the bathroom," I say.

"I never go down there," she says, flinching. "It's just too creepy."

17

THE MEDICAL EXAMINER

I will praise thee; for I am fearfully and wonderfully made.
—Psalm 139:14

THE MEDICAL EXAMINER IS a large man with a round, pleasant face. Dressed in a white, short-sleeved shirt, he will be with us for the night in the morgue, examining body parts as they are brought in, identifying them, and placing them like shattered puzzle pieces on one of the bare stainless steel tables. As I look at him, I realize that I am taking him in, holding him up like a curiosity in the light, turning him this way and that—much like he will be studying the bones and flesh that are destined to appear before us. He will try to place these fragments in the context of the human body, while I try to place him in the context of the human psyche. *Who could do his work?* I wonder. *Who could examine dead bodies, day after day, trying to determine cause of death, time of death?* I look, vaguely, for signs of oddity in his presence, but he seems more like a friendly visitor from Minnesota than a seasoned medical examiner from New York City.

When I report to the Temporary Morgue for my shift, I'm told the medical examiner is sleeping. It has been a quiet evening. This is difficult for many reasons. It is April, and the recovery process is slowing dramatically. With it, a growing determination to find something, anything, of human remains hangs heavily in the air. When hours go by and not a shred of a body is found, spirits sag and the night hours crawl. Like the endless drip of a leaky faucet, time moves—slowly—but each dripping second frays the nerves. The pressure builds, and then . . . nothing. Nothing. Just the hum of machines and the silent dance of men raking, raking the dust without ceasing, looking for what feels like a needle in a smoldering haystack. Only it is not a needle buried in the dust but the splintered bodies of brothers and sisters, mothers and fathers, sons and daughters.

After several quiet hours, a few small bags of remains and a lone fireman's boot are brought into the narrow trailer. As they are placed gently on one of the two receiving tables, the room begins to come alive. Someone flips on the fluorescent light; we blink for a moment, adjusting to the sudden brightness and the activity. It is 3:30 in the morning. Tired workers get up from the hard folding chairs on which they have been dozing and stretch. An EMT goes to wake the medical examiner, who is sleeping in an adjacent trailer. After a few minutes, he appears, walking heavily into the small space without a word. Now everything snaps into sharp focus. We take our places and begin what has become a familiar routine. I feel myself take a deep breath. The crime scene investigator is ready to photograph what has been recovered—evidence of the crime which took place some seven months ago—and an EMT stands by with the log in which each recovery is recorded by hand. I am there, too, to offer what little blessing I can over these broken bits of humanity.

— We watch in silence as the medical examiner begins with the boot. He takes it carefully in his large hands, and what he does next makes me suck an involuntary breath between my teeth. He puts the boot to his nose and matter-of-factly sniffs. Then he sniffs it again. "No," he says without expression. "No remains in here." "Are you sure?" someone asks. "I'd be able to smell decay," he answers. He puts the boot gently aside, and I see him give a small, respectful nod to the fireman standing by. As their eyes meet, I notice that the medical examiner is not without emotion, he is bone weary. Literally. Without a word he moves on to one of the small red plastic bags. Again the room is silent, motionless. He extracts from the bag what looks to be a four-inch piece of muddy cloth—only it is not cloth, it is tissue. "Human tissue," he says purposefully. "Site unspecified." The crime scene investigator steps up to the table to photograph the remains; it is recorded in the log with the date, time, and description. I understand that my blessing will have to wait until all the bags are opened. This has become the custom in these last days of the recovery process.

The medical examiner moves on to the next bag. Like a magician preparing to pull a rabbit from a hat, he carefully opens the bag while we wait to see what he will extract. Voilà. This time it is a perfect piece of rib, impossibly elegant, delicately curved and pure white, as if it had been meticulously scrubbed. It is about eight inches long. "Human rib," the M.E. announces without looking up, but I notice that his voice has softened ever so slightly, as have his features. Pausing, he holds the bone gently in his thick fingers, bringing it up to eye level. His expression is one of utter appreciation and reverence, like that of someone who is seeing a familiar but magnificent piece of art up close for the first time. "Look at this," he says to no one in particular. "It is brilliantly constructed. See the curve right here? See how it is bent inward just a little? This not only holds the muscles in place but it also protects the organs. It is pure genius."

I don't know if he is a religious man, but the room has become a sanctuary. I watch him in wonder. The contrast between his fleshy fingers and the graceful arc of the naked rib is almost too much to bear. Does he see that there is light streaming from what he holds in his hand? Does anyone else see this? His face is enraptured, like a child's. I am struck by his reverence but I also have the impulse to snatch the rib from him, to run from the trailer with the bone in my hand, screaming, "Here it is! Here it is! Whoever you are, I have your rib!" I want desperately to put it back in the body from which it came. It feels terribly wrong to have this piece of humanity, exposed and broken before us in this way. Something so private should not be viewed under the harsh glare of a fluorescent light, no matter how respectfully it is handled. For some reason, I feel ashamed; and I keep thinking that someone must have reached inside somebody else, dug his fingers into another's side, and extracted this something that didn't belong to him. I picture this body whole, perfect, but with a shaft of brilliant light pouring from the wound. *Put it back,* I keep repeating to myself. Trouble is, there is nowhere to put it. There is no body waiting for it, save the one I see in my mind, floating, forgiving, patient. Still, I want the medical examiner, with all his knowledge and appreciation, with his gentle, chubby fingers and his artist's eye, to find a way to return it to its rightful owner.

We are fearfully and wonderfully made, I hear in my head, and I am filled with awe. But, more than that, I am painfully aware that this perfect rib belonged to Someone. A specific Someone with a specific life and history and future that did not include dying on September 11. This rib is not art. It is not science. It is not a relic. It is evidence of a life that is no more. It bears the echo of sorrow and the DNA of generations past. It is a life that will not be repeated, replicated, replaced.

I look up just as the medical examiner gives me a nod. His work for the moment is done, while mine is just beginning. I look around the room and indicate, softly, that it is now time to offer a blessing on the remains. As always, the six or seven men and women who are gathered there, shoulder to shoulder, remove their hats and bow their heads. It is an act that always moves me. Contrary to what one may think, after so many months, it never feels routine or obligatory, just as the silence in the room never feels impatient or merely tolerant. It is filled with an intuitive awareness of Something Greater than ourselves. In this act of blessing remains, we are remembering something essential about being human, namely that life matters. It matters how we live and how we die, and how we are treated when we are dead. It means that *we* matter and, more important, that someone will remember that we matter. Honoring the dead is an inherently stubborn affirmation of life. And when you are surrounded by death, this may be the only lifeline available.

"Dear Lord," I begin. "You alone know to whom these parts belong. You knit the tissue before us, perfectly integrating it into the body. You placed this rib just so to give structure and form to one that once knew life. You know the foot that wore this boot that walked into hell for the sake of another human being and emerged into paradise. We commend these persons to your care. Receive them into the arms of your mercy, comfort the families who mourn them, and bless those who toil night and day so that others might be granted some small measure of peace. In your holy name we pray. Amen."

With that, hats are returned to heads, feet begin to shuffle out of the morgue into the night, and the stars, while invisible and silent, bear witness.

18

MAY 6, 2002

I T IS JUST BEFORE midnight when I arrive on-site. I pull my car into the small lot in front of the morgue. The roads are open to the public now, which makes driving easier, at least for these late-night shifts. The priest I am relieving looks tired. Our eyes meet, but only briefly. I recognize in him that familiar feeling of being glad the next chaplain has arrived, yet finding it difficult to leave. Where to go from here? Where do we ever go from here? We exchange few words. He tells me that it has been a quiet night, says his good-byes, then disappears into the city beyond the site.

I introduce myself to the two EMTs who are sitting side by side at a long folding table with their heads down. They smile sleepily but obviously don't feel like talking. Talking has dwindled, along with the recovery of remains. Even the desire to connect, to form some sort of bond, seems to have faded. I flip through the book in which the remains are logged. It is clear from the entries that the recovery efforts are yielding very little now—a bone fragment, a piece of tissue . . . It crosses my mind that it is going to be a very long, quiet night.

I step outside and survey the site. The cool air reminds me of the first night I spent here, in early October; but what I see is very different. Instead of the seemingly insurmountable pile, smoldering against a backdrop of shattered buildings, there is an increasingly neat pit. For a while, I watch the firemen raking through the dirt. They are moving meticulously, steadily. It is mesmerizing to watch them. "Like a ballet" is how someone described it in the newspaper recently. *Maybe,* I think. *But if it is, it is a strange and silent dance with death.*

I wonder how much longer I will be here. How much longer any of us will be here, raking, clearing, hoping, blessing, standing by, bearing witness. The end date for the recovery effort floats about in conversations. End of May? June? It is a curious feeling. When our work is done here, who will recover *us*? Who will look for us beneath the rubble of these months? Who will sift through the dirt searching for pieces of us, the bits and particles of who we were? Who will piece us back together; who will bless?

The night is just beginning, and there will be time for pondering such questions. The problem is we do not yet know we have been shattered. It's too early. We still think that we are the same people. We do not know that parts of us will be found on the tops of buildings, and in debris at Fresh Kills, and in manholes five years later. It is too early to know that every new discovery, no matter how many years later, no matter where we are, will break us a little. Every new bit recovered will prompt us to close our eyes and to whisper a prayer. We will look toward the heavens. We will see the bones before us. We will surround them with light. And, somewhere, ethereal men and women will remove their hats, bow their heads, and wait for the blessing that is sure to come.

19

REENTRY

I'M NOT SURE WHEN I stopped saying a prayer every time I saw an airplane, when I stopped squinting my eyes and extending my hand to give the illusion that I was holding the plane in my palm or balancing it on the tip of my finger, supporting it, guiding it. At some point, I must have stopped whispering, "Please, dear God, keep them aloft. Don't let them fall," but I couldn't tell you when. It used to be that I would look hard at every plane that crossed the sky, anxiously watching for any hint of trouble, expecting at any moment that it would take a treacherous and sudden turn—toward the city, toward the ground, toward certain death. I'm aware that I have stopped doing this, although an involuntary "Please, God, please," will still slip out every once in a while.

In the same way, I would shudder involuntarily every time I'd see a clump of leaves or debris on the side of the road as I drove. For a split second, I would be sure that I was seeing remains out of the corner of my eye. A discarded shoe or a scrap of muddy material would make me hit my brakes or jerk my head around. *What was that?* I would wonder. *Did I see something? Was that a torso? A limb? Is that decay I smell?* Strangely, I did not see human remains in animals killed along the road— these were recognizable—but I know that my heart sagged more than usual with each stiff raccoon or motionless squirrel I passed.

Now, years later, the dead I encounter are all intact, whole, known, and for the most part beloved by someone. The dead are those who have died on hospice, or whose funerals I have been asked to officiate. From time to time, the dead belong to my family. Death continues to come, but it is understandable, the dead recognizable. We usually know when and how they died; sometimes we are there. We can say our good-byes, we can bury them or cremate them, we can scatter their ashes, we can visit their graves. We can honor them one by one, which is enough to bear. Whether death comes as a result of disease or an accident, whether it is a suicide or a birth defect, most of us can eventually accept it.

What makes the deaths of September 11 so difficult is clearly the violent, communal, and very public way in which people perished, as well as the lack of recognizable remains. The world itself became unrecognizable on that beautiful blue morning. When the sky went black and the world went white with ash, it felt apocalyptic. Cultures, races, walks of life could hardly be distinguished. We watched them walk, shattered and bloodied, covered in debris and death. Shell-shocked and broken, all seemed to know that they themselves could be the ash that was covering their skin, their clothes, their identities, their spirits. Those who could, walked. They walked away from death. They walked toward life. They walked because there was nothing else to do but keep moving. And as they walked, they encountered the kindness and courage of strangers, reminding them of who they were, and of who they had been before the world went mad. But, at some point, they would have to stop moving, and that's when the thinking and the questioning—and the trauma—would really begin.

What do we do with those events for which there are no easy answers? In the months following the attacks of September 11, churches, synagogues, and houses of worship experienced a surge in attendance. People were looking for comfort, for hope, for an explanation to make sense of things, and they were looking in the places that stood for Order and Meaning. Who was in charge? If there was a God, how could He/She let this happen?

One of the most moving and poignant responses to the question of God's absence in the presence of suffering is recounted by Elie Wiesel in his autobiography, entitled *Night*. As he was forced to watch a young boy hang from the gallows of a concentration camp, dying a slow, torturous death, a prisoner in the crowd cried out: "Where is God now?" Wiesel writes, "And I heard a voice within me answer him: 'Where is He? Here He is—He is hanging here on this gallows.'"

Why do terrible things happen? Perhaps they happen not because God refuses to act in human history but because we refuse to act humanely. We are children running with expensive watches, with scissors, with the power to break and to hurt, to squander and to maim. We have the freedom to make terrible choices or to aspire toward holiness. And if we continue to point to the absence of God in the presence of evil, we will never take responsibility for our own actions, nor will we discover the God-ever-present, whose heart continues to break with ours.

Tragedy, heartbreak, illness, death—all of these place us squarely at the crossroads of existential and spiritual growth. What we do with the challenges that are sure to come is up to us. Most of us live our lives making deals with God or the Universe, consciously or unconsciously praying for answers to our prayers in exchange for the promise to do better, to be better, to try harder, to be more loving, more generous, more devoted. This is understandable, but it doesn't really get us anywhere in the long run, because some prayers will appear to get answered and some will not. The truth is that we are fragile, finite creatures. We get sick, we get injured, we hurt one another, we die. We fill our natural world, and our bodies, with toxins and wonder why there are more cancers, more illnesses. We hoard our wealth and our resources and wonder why there is resentment and violence. In essence, many of us go along just fine, without much thought about God or meaning, until the other shoe drops and we find ourselves in trouble, like a gambler who has played his last bad card.

We have another choice. Meister Eckehart, the thirteenth-century German mystic, wrote, "If the only prayer you prayed in your whole life is 'Thank you,' that would suffice." Thank you. More than acceptance—gratitude. It is a difficult path. What does this mean in the face of tragedy? Does it mean that we should be glad when terrible things happen? Obviously not. But to live with the kind of faith that does not depend on life going well is to live freely. And the only way to do this is to connect deeply to the constant, humming vibration of the Universe, the Song that never wavers, that which sings Love, only Love. That same pulse emanates from our own hearts if we are still enough to listen. But if this were easy, we would all be enlightened.

It is nearly impossible to feel gratitude, to feel loved by God or anyone else if we are stuck on the question of Why? Why did this terrible thing happen—to me, to my loved one, to the world? The question itself can leave us feeling persecuted, victimized, punished even. But if instead we are able to accept the ambiguities inherent in life, and to search for that which will help our spirits grow—namely ways to see beauty, avenues to experience love, expressions of creativity—we will find some traction, some grit to keep us from sliding off the cliff of despair.

Viktor Frankl, the Viennese psychiatrist, author, and Holocaust survivor, brilliantly addresses this in his magnificent work *Man's Search for Meaning*. As he lived through the concentration camps of World War II, it became clear to him that those who survived as human beings, those who survived spiritually, even if they were murdered, were those who could still feel love for another, who could still marvel at beauty, or whose creativity still yearned for expression in the world. Frankl's love for his wife (who he later learned had died in one of the camps) and his fervent desire to complete his work on Logotherapy helped him to hold on to his identity as a human being and as a unique soul. Even in the midst of great suffering, and after witnessing the worst in human nature, Frankl's spirit prevailed.

It is tempting to hear someone's tragic story and then begin to interpret it for her. We want to make things better, we want to have everything make sense, we want the pain resolved. But the truth is that it is the sufferer who must begin the search for and the discovery of meaning. Each soul has its own work to do. We each have a story that is ours alone. And if we have the courage to stand on the abyss of meaninglessness, looking not for reasons but for the truth of our own belovedness, then our suffering will be assuaged, and life will again have wonder and beauty.

Many years ago, I met a woman who beautifully illustrated how one can overcome suffering by finding meaning in her pain. Her husband was a retired minister, and they attended the first church I served after my ordination. She and her husband were both beloved by the church and valued for their insights and contributions; but there was something about Thelma that drew people to her. She radiated warmth and gentleness, welcoming anyone who needed a little love, a little understanding. She was wonderfully maternal, the mother or grandmother you always wanted.

When I met her, I assumed that she had raised her family and was enjoying grandchildren. But when I asked about her children, she smiled and said, "Oh, no. We were never able to have children of our own."

"I'm sorry," I stammered. "That must have been difficult for you."

"Well," she began, "it was hard in the beginning, certainly. But when I look back at all the children I have mothered, all the little ones who needed love, I realize that I could never have been there for them in the same way if I had had my own children. You see," she continued, her face aglow, "I am really the mother of more children than I ever could have imagined. God has truly blessed me."

Thelma's ability to interpret and then transmute her suffering made a deep impression on me. I will never forget that simple exchange or the look in her eyes as she spoke. I was a twenty-six-year-old, single, newly ordained clergywoman, and she was a woman in her eighties, married for over fifty years to her minister husband. Among the things she taught me that day was this: Life can be hard, but how we feel about the things that happen in life can evolve and change. Over time, as our lives unfold, we may understand them differently, we may become aware of the blessings that accompanied the hardships, and this may well transform the way in which we think about our lives. But the journey is ours; the discoveries to be made must be made by us alone if they are to be genuine. I could not have told Thelma, for instance, how her childlessness was actually a blessing to many others; this would have been cruel and insensitive. But *she* could tell me this; the insight, the spiritual growth, was hers.

We can walk with one another, we can support one another, and we are called to do so. But we dare not ever say to one in pain, "Well, this happened because of that, and that happened because of this." Perhaps the only thing we can do is to be present and to ask, "What do you think this means for your life? How do you want to live in light of what has happened? Is there a way to feel, even now, whole, loved, blessed?"

Working with the dying has taught me a great deal about the individual journey, and about the challenge of changing oneself in light of unchangeable circumstances. As our medical professionals seek to alleviate the symptoms of disease—the pain, the wounds, the indignities suffered by the body—the Spirit, too, calls for assistance to ease its suffering. The difference is, there are things we can do *to* a body. We can administer morphine, we can change dressings, we can position, we can feed. But the Spirit is required to participate in its healing; it cannot passively be acted upon. No chaplain, no healer, however powerful, can "fix" someone unless he or she is willing to be "fixed." There have been times when nurses have become exasperated with a patient, with seeing his or her spiritual and emotional suffering, and have said to me, "You've got to *do* something!" as if I could heal the spiritual wound with the equivalent of an antibiotic. Unfortunately, we are not made this way. Even Jesus was known to ask the curious question of those who came for healing, "Do you *want* to be well?" It's like the old joke: How many therapists does it take to change a lightbulb? Answer: Just one—but the lightbulb has to want to change.

One of the most honest encounters I have had with a hospice patient involved a woman I'll call Ellen. Ellen was an elderly woman who had been married twice, outliving both of her husbands. One of her daughters had died several years before of cancer, and the other, no matter how attentive, could never seem to do enough for her in Ellen's mind. To make matters more complicated, Ellen's grandson, to whom she had been very close, was now estranged from her. "You've got to help her find peace," the nurse practically ordered me.

I'm not so sure that this lightbulb, this dear, stubborn old patient wanted to change. After hearing her story, and listening to her plaintive cry of how nothing could give her joy while this break with her grandson continued, and after making suggestions, all of which she rejected, I finally asked her: "Okay, Ellen. If we cannot convince your grandson to let go of his anger and to reconcile with you, what might bring you peace?" I was thinking that she might be able to find it in her heart to forgive him or to accept the fact that healing might come sometime in the future, though perhaps not while she was alive, or that she might express gratitude for the daughter, who tended to her night and day. Instead, she answered incredulously, with eyes wide: "Peace? I don't *want* to be at peace." And that was the simple truth.

I laughed and said, "Ellen, that is perhaps the most honest thing anyone has ever said to me. Good for you." It occurred to me that she did not want to be at peace with her grandson, or with herself, because then she would have to deal with the fact that she was dying. She was terrified to let go of her hurt and her anger because she felt she would have no other branch on which to hold, nothing else to rage against, and therefore she would die. The idea of finding peace, of surrendering, frightened her because she knew intuitively that her life would change, that she would change. Most of us are not that honest.

For the terminally ill, for those who know their time is limited, there are often opportunities for spiritual growth that are not available to those who die suddenly. Clearly, we do not have to be facing death to make peace with our loved ones, with ourselves, or with our understanding of the Divine. We do not have to be dying to express love for another, or to aspire toward the experience of feeling loved. But when death looms on the horizon, when we know it is coming, our time frame is condensed, and we more naturally turn our minds to questions of meaning.

For many, there is also regret—regret that we did not live up to our own expectations, that our lives were not fulfilled or fulfilling. And, for some of us, there is anguish, emanating from a deep yearning to make sense of things, to feel connected in that primal way to Something Greater than ourselves, to be healed of our innate loneliness, and to know in our hearts that we are not alone, that we will not *be* alone, and that we are loved.

As the shock of our mortality begins to wear off, some will begin their journey toward meaning, acceptance, wisdom, and peace. It is both a tuning in and a turning toward Ultimate Meaning. For some, it will be like moving toward what is dear and familiar, like returning from a long trip. Others will experience a single-mindedness of purpose, a focus on what is ahead, and their pace will quicken, like that of a horse to the barn, as they near the completion of this life. But all of us will one day discover for ourselves where the road will lead, what awaits us, and what it is—finally—to surrender fully to the pulse of Life. As in birth, when we were pushed along by the contractions of our mothers' wombs into the bright unknown, so in death we will be moved by forces beyond our control.

What awaits, we cannot know, but I have witnessed the passing of some who have courageously embraced this journey. There, an unmistakable beam of light could be seen crossing the face, a look of pleasant surprise, a dawning recognition in the eyes of Something or Someone we have yet to fathom. For these, the final breath is more like a sigh of contentment.

Perhaps it is not a coincidence, then, that one of the most common things people say when they are dying is "I want to go home." They may utter this lying in the same bed in the same house that they have lived in for fifty years; they may whisper this in the arms of a lifelong love; they may smile kindly at the adult child who does not understand. "I'm tired and I want to go home," they say over and over. Being told they *are* home offers no consolation—for the home of which the dying speak begins with a capital *H*. It is the Home of the Spirit. They know it, they feel it, they move toward it, they welcome it. What *it* signifies is complete connection, complete at-homeness. More than union, it is reunion.

To walk with the dying is to glimpse what it means to go Home. It is to listen for the Voice that seems to call them, the Voice we ourselves yearn to hear—a Voice of comfort, of love, of welcome. It is the Voice that leads to the open arms of the Mother who is always waiting for us, always loving us. It is the accelerated journey toward Mystery. Once we arrive, perhaps we will discover that we have, in fact, always been Home.

20

LIVING WITH GHOSTS

ONE OF THE CENTRAL stories of my childhood has nothing in a way to do with me but rather with the ghost of someone I never met. Her presence permeated our home, like the soft fragrance left behind by a beautiful woman, giving one the impression that she had just been there, had just gone, slipping silently out the door so as not to cause a fuss—my father's mother. She died when my dad was nine years old from an illness never fully understood or diagnosed, altering his childhood and his life, and in turn my childhood and my life, in innumerable ways. She was thirty-four, petite and soft-spoken, with rivers of dark brown hair and shining black-brown eyes. She had deep dimples that framed her small face like parentheses or cupped hands, and pretty lips whose bell-shaped curve hinted at a slight overbite. It had the pleasing effect of bringing her whole face forward, like she was about to tell a secret or break into a conspiratorial giggle. Her eyes, and that imperfect smile, made her somehow accessible and present, while the reality of her absence made her perpetually mysterious.

As a child, I would stare at the few pictures we had of her. One, taken for her high school graduation, shows her sitting demurely with legs crossed in a white sailor suit, a style popular in the twenties. Her hair is parted in the middle and neatly arranged in tight curls that encircle her head in a mahogany halo and spill softly down her cheeks. There are two shots of her in her wedding gown, one by herself and one with my grandfather. She appears tiny and vibrant next to his athletic, six-foot frame. A lace cap rests on her twenty-year-old forehead, accentuating eyes that I still search—for their secrets, for my father, for my DNA.

My grandfather, on the other hand, is staring into the camera with the uncomplicated ease of a happy groom. As I look at him, I bring the cache of my childhood memories— the sound of his voice, the smell of Old Spice on his neck, the weight of his body reclining in a chair. He is young and old at the same time for me. In the groom of twenty-nine, I see the blueprint for the seventy-year-old man I knew as a grandfather. I accept the parts of him I do not know, will never know, because he exists in my tactile memory. But the young woman beside him is another story. She, too, exists in memory—but not mine. She exists in the memory of my father. She was his mother but never my grandmother. She was real to him. She *belonged* to him. She birthed him and knew him and counted his toes and brushed her lips on his baby head. She quietly delighted in his perfection in the secret way that mothers do; she fretted over him, grieved for him, and bore the heartache of knowing he would suffer when she died. She could not spare him that.

Of course, this is my projection. I have a son, and I know what it is to love him fiercely. If I died, what would he remember of me? What would he tell his children? What would shatter, what would shift, what could never be healed? And what perception of me would he protect, embellish, idealize? It is excruciating to consider.

Maybe this is why the saddest picture for me is a snapshot taken not long before my grandmother died. Again she is standing next to my grandfather; but this time, instead of a wedding gown, she is wearing a simple cotton dress. It reveals the womanly curves she has acquired in the years since her wedding photo. She is no longer a teenager or a bride. Her hair is less tamed, less coiffed, exuding an unruly freedom that complements the laughter in her eyes. Her hands rest on the small shoulders of my father and his sister, both of whom are squinting into what appears to be an afternoon sun. They are smiling, unaware of the shadow that has yet to fall upon their lives.

I stare at the photo, and I am mesmerized. I am older now than she was when she died. Even in dream, she could not have imagined me, could not have fathomed the cosmic spool of genetic thread that would continue to unravel across the universe with or without her. She barely had time to memorize her children's features, teach them to tie their shoes, pray that they would remember her, remember the sound of her voice, her smell, remember that she loved them. I think that, if I look long enough, I will be able to hear her voice, that she will reveal some essential key to who I am, to who my father is, and that together we can heal him.

The story of her death is so real to me that sometimes I forget I was not there. It happened in the summer of 1944. Victory over Japan was still a year away. Young men in new uniforms were armed with purpose and bravery and patriotism and bravado. Most went willingly to war, enthusiastically forging their fates and the fate of the world through sacrifice and service. While some began their journeys to Europe, or the Pacific Theater, or Hawaii, others would be dying, wounded, or missing around the globe. Stars designating their fates would appear in the windows of what seemed to be every other home—blue for active duty, gold for killed in action, silver for the wounded. A change in the window would prompt neighbors to bow their heads, to lower their voices out of respect, or to offer a simple word of condolence. Children would stop playing to solemnly salute.

Everyone accepted the fact that the lives of men were hanging as precariously as those felt stars, stars that made each street a constellation of pride and pain. But what was also understood, and perhaps taken for granted, was that within those homes were women keeping the lives of children safe and ordered. The enemy was somewhere very far away, farther even than the crackly voice on the radio heard in the safety of one's living room—at least for everyone else.

For my father, the enemy crept quietly into his home on an August morning. While other nine-year-old boys were meeting at the baseball diamond to lazily run the bases, or argue over balls and strikes, or check their pockets for a few pennies to buy an egg cream, my dad was watching his mother's draped body being carried out of the house. There would be no star in the window, no symbol to give the neighbors pause. Every time he spoke of this, his voice would break with the pain, with the wound that would never heal.

But that is his story. Those are his images.

I do not have the pain of his loss, but I have its ghost. I recognize it in the melancholy that my father drapes around his shoulders like a comfortable shawl. I recognize it in the same black-brown eyes that search for meaning, that hunger after the unknown, that are impenetrable and accessible at the same time. Because he lost her—his mother, Edythe, my *real* grandmother, as he often referred to her—he allowed himself to search for her. We all searched for her. And the search took the form of candlelight séances, spiritual exploration, and the belief that life is an ongoing journey.

Growing up, I could not see my father apart from this loss. He existed in the world as someone with a broken heart—but what seeped through those cracks, strangely enough, was something magical. His brokenness made him tender and imaginative. It loosened up the joints of his psyche and opened him (and us) to the reality of things we could not see. Refracted light, like a prism, spilled out of him, dappling and illuminating our lives with glimmers of the mystical; and because he had the courage not to plug the holes, life was fluid and exciting and full of possibilities. Summoning the dead was an adventure, life was an adventure; and death was just a labyrinth that would lead us to Her.

The problem was, I wanted to fix him. I wanted to take

away the tears that threatened to flow with the light, the tears that pooled just below the surface. In short, I wanted him to have his mother back.

It makes sense, then, that I would find myself working as a hospice chaplain. The hardest cases for me, not surprisingly, were those involving children—either those who were dying or those with a parent who was dying. I both dreaded being the one who might break the news to a child that his or her parent had died and guarded it as a sacred privilege. "Speak to me, Edythe," I would whisper. "Give me the words you would have wanted your little boy to hear. Help me. Guide me. Strengthen me for this task." Making my way into the room of such a child, I would picture my grandmother already there, consoling the ghost of the parent who now yearned to console the child.

Living with the ghost of my grandmother made me more comfortable with death, perhaps, than some. On the one hand, I knew that death was real, that it came to the young and the old alike, that it was painful to bear. But I was also acutely aware of its inherent ability to point to the Unknown. Life, death, and mystery were a braided cord embedded in my genetic code, interlacing my cells and sinews, tethering me to the earth, connecting me to stardust.

Something of this cosmic cord was revealed in the early hours of an August morning when Edythe's great-granddaughter Catherine Elizabeth took her first lungful of air. Perhaps they had just been conversing about how the light looked on earth as compared with the Other World and how the human experience offered unique lessons. Then, when the exact hour and minute had finally arrived, the perfect timing (as all births are perfectly timed), I'd like to think the kindred souls embraced.

"It's time," said one.

"I'm not sure I'm ready," said the other.

"I will be with you," the first reassured, gently.

"Will I feel you in the wind and the sun? Will I find you in the stars?"

"Yes, I will be there . . . and in the hum of your mother's heart . . . and in the brush of her lips on your head."

"Where else?"

"Look for me in the eyes of my son, eyes that have softened like melted chocolate; once they burned with fire."

"I will bring your light."

WHEN I CALLED my father at four in the morning to tell him of Catherine's arrival, he asked me if I knew what day it was. Gazing down at my daughter's face, at the perfect bud of her mouth, the roundness of her cheeks, and the dimples that were already obvious, I told him that I really had no idea. All I knew was that my little dark-haired goddess had finally arrived, three weeks late and a whopping nine and a half pounds.

"It's the day my mother died," he told me softly. "In fact, it was forty-nine years ago today."

"Oh, Dad, I'm so sorry," I said, snapping out of my dreamy haze. Instinctively, I pressed my new daughter to my breast, as if to fend off the invisible arms that were waiting to carry her away.

"No, don't be sorry," he said genuinely. "This day has always been hard for me, but now it's been transformed. I can't help but feel that it is a gift from my mother, as though she is releasing me from the sadness and the pain of this day. From here on out, I can no longer think of this as just the day she died because it is also the birthday of my granddaughter, her great-granddaughter." Then, as he paused, the flicker of stars at dawn, of morning light, began to seep into his voice. It was the familiar sound of a new adventure, a fragment uncovered, an invitation. I could hear him smile, could feel the embers stirring in his eyes. "Do you think they passed each other on the way down?" he asked.

I may never be able to heal my father, and it could be that he does not want to be healed. Maybe for him, the ghost that has accompanied him all these years speaks not of absence but of presence. Maybe he is moving toward her; maybe she has been there all along. For me, she speaks of the continuity of life. She is the whispered voice that says to embrace what is, to marvel at what I will never know, and to keep living.

21

DEATH OF A PSYCHIC

SUSPENDED BETWEEN EARTH AND sky, between the busy city sidewalks and the Great Beyond, I sat waiting my turn to see Yolana. Her apartment was perched on the edge of the East Side of Manhattan, tottering precariously near the Williamsburg Bridge and the East River, the FDR and the Roosevelt Island Tram. Getting there was not always easy, but once you were inside, the real journey began, and it was more than worth it.

Yolana was a gifted psychic, mother, grandmother, and free spirit. Once dubbed the "Queen of Psychics," she became famous for helping the NYPD solve difficult cases. Though she became quite renowned through the years, she remained ever herself—down-to-earth, wonderfully irreverent, deeply spiritual, loving, and genuinely concerned. She welcomed the seeker, she tolerated the worried, she held court with the famous. She mingled comfortably with the homeless (having been there once herself long ago). A healer and a mystic, she was a woman who had seen it all, who had suffered greatly and prevailed, and who continued to find it in herself to keep helping those who sought out her extraordinary gift.

What brought me to her initially was not a deep spiritual quest but rather the simple heartbreak of a lost cat. Our cat, Miles, had been missing for nearly two weeks, and I was desperate to find him. Miles, of Russian blue descent, was a pauper prince among cats, one who barely escaped being stoned to death as a kitten. Miles, plush and gorgeous, and unaware of his nobility. He was the most loving and gentle cat I have ever known, and magical, too. How he came to us is now part of our family lore; how he returned to us is part of the Mystery.

Before we got him, we had asked the children what kind of cat they thought they might like. My daughter wanted a white cat—hence came Stella. My three-year-old son insisted he needed a blue cat. He would not be deterred when we told him there was really no such thing as a blue cat. Instead, he stubbornly furrowed his brow and announced that, if his sister could choose a white one, he could pick a blue one. We sighed, hoping that he would forget his quest for the blue cat when presented with so many other choices. When we arrived at the shelter in Yonkers, Alex took one look at Miles, with his distinctly blue-gray fur and emerald eyes, and triumphantly carried him home.

Now, somehow, our magical cat was gone. My husband and I canvassed our neighborhood, plastering it with flyers. We walked and walked calling his name, we took out a lost-and-found ad in the paper, we rang the local shelters, we knocked on countless doors. With each passing day, we grew more despondent, envisioning Miles injured and unable to get home or, worse still, dead on the side of some unknown road.

For some reason, I just could not believe that he was gone for good, and I racked my mind to think of what else we could do to find Miles. Then, I thought of Yolana. I had never met her, but I had been fascinated with the idea of seeing her someday. She was the mother of my chiropractor, Dr. Michael Bard, a man whose own intuitive gifts are evident in his healing hands and his ability to tune in to his patients, to find the blockages and free them. His physical adjustments often seem to carry with them an emotional component. This was never more evident to me than when I was doing my work at the morgue downtown. When I had my first appointment with Dr. Bard after beginning that work, I started to weep as he adjusted me. As he freed my neck and my back, I realized how much sadness I was carrying in my body, how much pain I was literally shouldering. As my body began to unlock, my spirit exhaled—and I was profoundly grateful for the unburdening.

When he casually told me about his mother being a psychic, something resonated. The world of mystics and mediums, of psychics and spiritual advisers was not strange to me—in fact, it was completely familiar and comfortable. Odd as it may sound, one of my favorite family activities when I was growing up was having a Saturday night séance. As early as I can remember, we would gather around the dining room table, light a candle, say a prayer, and sit as my father began to channel messages from a world we could not see. What else was there to do in Ohio? I assumed everybody did this. I took it for granted that one could communicate with the dead, that messages for the living could be received, and that this was a natural part of life. My father usually downplayed his psychic abilities, but he could not deny the gift he had for "seeing" or for receiving images from the Unknown. He considered himself a vessel for collecting the messages that came through and said that my mother was the "generator" of spiritual energy. I guess we children were there to experience the mystery and to be the open channels of belief, hope, trust. This was no parlor game; it was more like taking a spiritual hike into the wild. My father was the guide—pushing, seeking, exploring—and we followed happily along, feeling safe and full of wonder in his care.

So natural was it for us to gather as a family in this way that I would sometimes forget that not everyone believed in such spiritual exercises. On one occasion, for example, my parents were experimenting with automatic writing, in which two people hold the same pen, allowing the energy to flow through them to guide the written message. In the middle of this, the phone rang, and I went to answer it. It was my grandmother, my mother's mother—a deeply religious woman, a Methodist, who didn't believe in drinking, dancing, or card playing, much less communicating with the dead. She had an abiding faith and a no-nonsense attitude toward life. We never told her that my sister and I took classical ballet for ten years (because it was dancing), and we certainly could not have told her that we held court with the spirit world on a regular basis.

"What are you doing, honey?" she asked, when I answered the phone.

"Having a séance," I answered innocently in my six-year-old voice.

"*What?*" she gasped, certain that she had misunderstood.

"Drawing pictures," I replied calmly, without missing a beat. I had instantly recognized my mistake, as reflected in the wide-eyed expression of my mother, whose hand still rested on my father's, holding the pen. My recovery might have been a stretch, but it was as close as I could get to the truth.

Later, I came to realize how unique my parents were, how spiritually adventurous and curious, and how that love of spiritual exploration permeated our family life. We were never surprised by the noises or strange occurrences that happened frequently in our home. We accepted the fact that one of us might, at any time, have a mystical experience or an ethereal visitation in the night, and we looked forward to the animated discussion that was sure to follow around the dinner table the next day. The veneer that separated the world of spirit and the world of flesh seemed paper-thin at my house. If you could not see those who abided with you, you could certainly feel their presence (if you were open to it), and I always found that comforting. Pushing our noses to the glass between the seen and the unseen, between what we know and what we can only fathom, was not scary; it was simply how we lived.

It seemed quite natural, then, for me to turn to Yolana for help with Miles. I had observed my father on numerous occasions welcoming strangers who came to him for insights, for comfort, or for communion with their loved ones. He rarely shared the content of those sessions, over which he presided like a gentle sage or kindly confessor, and he would never accept any payment for his help. But I do know that whatever insights he might have offered were always accompanied by a fervent prayer for these people, for the pain that had prompted their visits, and for the healing of their hearts. Knowing my father, I am sure that he encouraged all who came to seek community in a church—ours or any other—because he is first and foremost a Christian man with a deep connection to Christ. He approaches the Scriptures and prayer the same way he approaches the world of spirit—with intelligence, enthusiasm, and humility.

This is not to say that we didn't also have some fun welcoming others to our séance table! I remember one night in particular when I was in high school. My then boyfriend, Scott, and I were sitting and chatting with my parents, as we so often did on the weekends. Scott was really more than a boyfriend—he was a member of our family. Our paternal grandfathers had worked together at the Cincinnati Gas and Electric Company long before we were born, and his great-aunt lived across the street from my grandparents. From the start, my parents adored Scott, and the feeling was mutual. Through the years we dated, it often seemed that he was as devoted to them as he was to me (a truth still evident in their ongoing friendship). The fact that he loved my mother's cooking and was fascinated by my father's psychic abilities didn't hurt. In short, he was the perfect captive audience.

On this night, we were having a discussion about life after death and whether our loved ones can still communicate with us after they have passed on. My parents had just returned from the funeral of my mother's cousin Phyllis, whose death had been ruled a suicide, though there was serious speculation that she had been murdered. Scott's grandfather (on his mother's side) had also died. "Would you like to see if he'll come through?" my father asked casually. "Sure," Scott answered somewhat nervously, inching his chair a little closer to mine.

The lights went out, the candle was lit, the prayers were said, and the adventure began. In semitrance, my father acknowledged the presence of a few spiritual guides who often appeared to him during these sessions—then he said, "Okay, Scott, I think I have your grandfather here." Without looking, I felt a ripple pass through Scott, an imperceptible wave of recognition, an acknowledgment of what the heart already knows. My father had never met this grandfather, had never seen a picture of him—yet he began to describe in great detail what the man looked like, down to the hair on his arms and hands, and the particular way he flicked his cigarette. I don't remember what else was said, but I do know that Scott was deeply moved by the experience, and by the reassurance that life does indeed go on.

When the session seemed to reach its natural conclusion, we continued to relax, talking softly in the flickering glow of the candle. The conversation drifted to my mother's cousin, to her untimely death and the suspicions surrounding it. My father had received powerful images while at Phyllis's funeral, even experiencing a physical push at one point, accompanied by a strong aural impression. "Despite the evidence to the contrary," he said, "my sense is that this was not a suicide." His eyes narrowed for a moment, as if squinting into the horizon of that world beyond for the answer. Then, just as the words left his mouth, there was a loud bang on our hall closet.

"See," my mother said, matter-of-factly. "That's Phyllis telling us you're right." My dad and I glanced over at the closet and nodded, as if pleasantly surprised by the unexpected appearance of our guest, in essence saying, "Oh, yes! There she is now."

"Wh-what?" asked Scott, looking as if he was about to spring from his chair. "What was that? What do you mean by saying that was Phyllis?"

"Well," said my mom, laughing a little, "I have Phyllis's nursing uniform in that closet—the one she was found in. In fact, it has a little of her blood on it."

Even in the candlelight, I could see Scott blanch. "But, what was that noise? Did something fall?"

"I don't think so," said my mom thoughtfully. "I think she was just letting us know that she's here and that she didn't kill herself. But I'll open the closet just to make sure."

My mother went over to the large hall closet and opened the sliding doors. She stood there like Vanna White pointing to the prize behind the curtain as the rest of us looked on. Everything was in place—nothing had fallen. The three of us—my mother, father, and I—started to giggle, realizing the nonchalance with which we had accepted the knock on the door as being a message from Phyllis. Scott just shook his head, dumbfounded. My parents and I still laugh when we think about that night—and I doubt Scott has ever forgotten it.

These early experiences taught me to be spiritually open, paving the way for my own mystical encounters. On numerous occasions through the years, I have had the experience of waking in the night to find a luminous figure near my bed or hovering over me. This usually startles me, causing me to cry out, just as it would if the shapes were real flesh-and-blood people. After the initial shock, when I realize what's happening, I always kick myself for reacting with such fear. For I know that no spiritual presence will ever hurt me; none are there to do me harm.

One of the most interesting visitations I had occurred a couple of years ago. It was late at night, and I was tossing and turning in bed. At that time, I was struggling with my career, my marriage, and my sense of purpose. As I rolled over for the umpteenth time, I was startled to find a man standing over me. He was dressed in a white button-down shirt and wore black horn-rimmed glasses. I could see his square jaw and the white hair that framed his bald head. He was bending near me, looking quite intense, angry even. The vibration of his words penetrated my ears, though I cannot say they were really audible by normal standards. He looked into my face and said, "You were made for more than this." I screamed—not once but (according to my husband) about five times. Thinking he was an intruder, I jumped out of bed and went to push him away. In doing so, I passed right through him—and when I did so, the name *Harry Denman* resonated in my head and in my chest.

Harry Denman. I hadn't heard or thought of that name since I was a child (I wasn't even sure who he was), and I had never seen a picture of the man. Later, I learned that he had been a Methodist evangelist known for his humility, his dedication to spreading the Gospel, and his lack of materialism.

My parents had heard him preach on several occasions in the 1960s, and I am sure that I was aware on some level of the impact he had on them. Still, Harry Denman? I was surprised by how that name came to me when I passed through the figure that filled my room like moonlight. And what did his words mean? I returned to bed and, strangely enough, immediately fell sound asleep.

The next morning, I could not wait to get to my computer. I Googled Harry Denman, and there, as I had anticipated, came the black-and-white image of a man in a coat and tie, with white hair, black glasses, and a square jaw. It was the first time I had ever seen a picture of him, but his face was exactly that of the ethereal figure I had seen in the night. "Harry," I whispered in wonder.

I contemplated why he might have come to me. I thought about his message. I felt completely honored by his visit. I am still trying to figure out what it is I am supposed to do here on earth, what exactly is that for which I have been made. But one thing is certain: I know I must keep growing, keep seeking. The last thing I want to do is irritate Harry, for he is quite a formidable force.

Around this time, I had a discussion with my five-year-old son about matters of life and death. He was going through a "worried" stage, contemplating the horrific reality that I will one day die. My children are more aware of death and mortality than many of their peers because of my work, both at hospice and at Ground Zero. Though I tried to reassure him that most likely he would be an old man when I died, and that even then I would be with him in his heart, he wasn't buying.

"But when you're dead, I won't be able to touch you," he said sadly. "It won't be the same. I might be able to see you, but I won't really have you with me. You'll be a spirit."

Curious, I asked him, "Well, Alex, have you ever seen a spirit?"

He paused for a moment and then said, "Yes."

"When?"

"Well," he continued matter-of-factly, "sometimes at night I see them all standing near my bed."

"Do you recognize anyone?"

"No."

"Does that scare you?" I asked, fascinated.

"Naw," he said, shrugging his shoulders. "If you don't know them, they don't really bother you. They just want to come and look at you."

A year or two later, Alex had little memory of this exchange, or of his nightly visitors.

I recognize that my own experiences as a child helped me to be more comfortable with death and contributed to my working with the dying. What I discovered is that seeing life as a spiritual journey transforms our perceptions about what is important, and opens our eyes to the guidance that we often seek but cannot perceive. And believing in the ongoingness of life gives strength and courage to the sojourner. With the dying and their families, I help to facilitate an exploration of their own beliefs, their own perceptions about life and death and the hereafter, and to find comfort in the interpretations of their experiences. Even those who don't believe in God or in life after death will often find peace in acknowledging that life is a mystery, and that death is a venture into the Unknowable.

And so, on a Friday night some twenty years after that time with Scott and my parents and Phyllis and the closet (and before my little visit with Harry), I found myself in the great Yolana's apartment. In many ways, it was like coming home. Her assistant opened the door and showed me in, directing me to a comfortable couch. As instructed, I had brought pictures of Miles and a blank cassette tape. The room was orderly and quiet, with large windows that overlooked the city below. On a glass table in front of me was a thick book of clippings and testimonials about Yolana. The faint scent of cigarette smoke danced invisibly in the air, mimicking all that cannot be seen but is present nonetheless. Sitting there fumbling with my pictures and my purse, I met the large, round eyes of Yolana's silver Persian cat, Samantha, who sauntered by me with a mixture of boredom and disdain. She seemed to imply that I was a guest there—and when Yolana was finished peering into the void on my behalf, I had to go home.

It had to be this way, I am sure. Because being in Yolana's presence not only opened the door to mystery but made one hunger for more. It was hard to leave her, she who could see, she who could make you feel utterly accepted, make you laugh at yourself, make you believe in what we cannot hold in our hands. Yolana, with her fiery red hair and her wandering eye, could peek behind the curtain of life and time, offering insights and guidance, and occasionally a word of greeting from the dead. If she made it too comfortable, who would ever leave?

When I took my place across the table from her in the small room in which she worked, she popped the cassette I had brought into a recorder, explaining that it was often difficult for people to remember what she told them. I realized, too, that this indicated her willingness to stand by what she said, the authenticity of her work, and the truth she tried to reveal. I explained why I was there and showed her Miles's picture. She studied it for a moment, brushing the photo lightly with her thumbs. Then she took my hand and held it over his picture.

"What do you feel?" she asked.

For a moment, I panicked, fearing I wouldn't feel anything at all. But then I allowed myself to be still inside, floating to the bottom of my center, like a penny thrown into a deep pool. I let go of everything except the awareness of my palm hovering but a few inches above the photograph of the creature I loved. Then I felt it—a force, an energy, invisible and yet clearly perceptible.

The feeling reminded me of an old magnetic tic-tac-toe game I used to have as a child. The round disks would bounce above one another on their wooden pegs, suspended invisibly by the like charge between them. I was fascinated by the way they would either snap together or push apart depending on what side of the magnet was used. It was a science lesson in how opposites attract and like charges repel, and a spiritual lesson in the reality and power of things we cannot see.

"I feel an almost magnetic force pushing my hand away," I replied sheepishly.

"That's right!" smiled Yolana, genuinely delighted by my

meager ability to feel something. "That's how you know he is alive. If you could not feel that life force in his picture, it would mean that he is dead." In the world of magnets, I guess you could say that his positive life energy was pushing against mine.

She then proceeded to tell me what had happened to Miles, how he came to be lost, and where he was spending his time. She gave me his exact location, including street name and description of the area, told me how to get him home and the day he would return. She said Miles could hear my husband and me calling him but didn't know which way to follow. This made sense since we often split up as we walked, calling to him from different directions. Without my having told her about them, she saw the "Lost" flyers we had posted and commented that it was smart of us not to list an amount for the reward offered. She reassured me that Miles was safely waiting out this time near a house owned by a particular family (which she named). Finally, she asked me why my car wasn't parked in the driveway—a detail that I had not given her—and said that Miles had become disoriented and was looking for it. My car was, in fact, at the shop getting minor repairs. She instructed me to pick it up as soon as I could, to call Miles from one particular spot, and to trust that he would be home from his adventure by Sunday.

The next day, Saturday, I did as Yolana instructed, picking up my car and parking it in the driveway. I then ventured through a wooded area at a bend in our road, one which I had never even noticed but which she had described perfectly. When I emerged on the other side of the woods, there was a house with a small sign saying the name of the family that she had given me. And, to my amazement, parked in their driveway was the exact make, model, and color of my car. "He's looking for your car," her voice whispered in my ear. Well, there it was. I called Miles as I walked from that house to my own, steadily marking a straight path with the echo of my words—*this direction, this way, follow me, Miles*—*come home.*

On Sunday morning, my husband opened the back door of the house, and there, to his utter amazement and joy, was Miles. I was upstairs when I heard him yell—then he came bolting up the stairs with our frightened blue prince in his arms. "Yolana," we both said as we looked at each other in astonishment.

Now, Yolana is dead. Even as I type those words, I cannot believe it. Yolana, with her husky voice and her gypsy smile and, most of all, with those eyes that could really see—gone. She managed to slip away—When? In the early-morning hours? In the evening? We will never know, and it doesn't matter anyway, because knowing will not bring her back.

When I got the call, I was leaving a funeral over which I had just presided. Hearing her son's voice on the other end of the phone, I quickly pulled over in my car. Little did I know that I had stopped on a hill in the cemetery overlooking the exact spot where Yolana would be buried a few days later. Of all the places to be, that's where I was. Now I wonder . . . if I had her gift of sight, would I have seen Yolana checking out her new grounds? Would I have seen her skipping about, light as a feather now, smiling, free, and pleasantly surprised, tossing back her head and chuckling at the thought that this soft, green ground, this new spring dirt could contain her? Maybe. At least I would like to think so.

When Yolana died, it felt like a door had been closed. No more peeking, no more crib notes to the unfolding story of your life. Her extraordinary gift was like a treasure map that only she could see, but one that she was willing to share—because the map, in essence, always pointed the seeker home to his or her own life, own truth, own self-understanding, own treasure trove of spiritual insights and beliefs. She could offer guidance, but mostly she offered presence; and in her presence, one felt alive with the possibility that Help was on the way.

To be with Yolana was to rest in the awareness that Something Greater exists, Something beyond our limited understanding, our limited vision. She gave what few could give, namely a glimpse into Mystery—into the promise that there is more to life than meets the eye. And this was balm for every anxious, curious, seeking, or broken spirit that came through her door. "Tell me, Yolana, that I'll find love, that I'll be okay, that my loved one's all right, that I'll make the right decisions in life." What a drain we must have been for her at times. And yet, she greeted each weird and wobbly soul with the same warmth and compassion, summoning from herself the very best she had, extracting from the Beyond whatever it was willing to give.

I saw Yolana on several other occasions over the course of about ten years. Always, she would offer reassurance and guidance. She provided loving and humorous insights about my children, she encouraged my impulse to write; and each time she would firmly instruct me to do more meditating, more praying, more developing of my faith and of my own spiritual identity. I considered her a spiritual guide and teacher, a companion on the journey, and a truth-teller of the most courageous kind. There are those who might think it odd that a Methodist minister would seek the counsel of a psychic. But from the days of the prophets, the interpreters of dreams, the sages, and the mystics, God has found ways to speak to a people still learning how to hear. Some, like Yolana, can listen better than others, tuning in to a frequency inaudible to most, and recognize God's voice. Some can feel the magnetic pull of invisible, living energy, or see angels in shapes of light, or hear God's primordial song in the lilt of nature—these often become our poets and artists and musicians. And some can teach the seeker how to hear.

People who are dying seem to tune in to this frequency more clearly. It is like a homing signal for the soul. People who are living, especially those who have lost a loved one, sometimes have a more difficult time hearing or experiencing it. While the bereaved yearn for reassurance, for connection to those they can no longer see or touch, the cry of the heart can, for a time, drown out that spiritual beacon. Some will seek out a person like Yolana to help make the connection for them. Others will be standing at the kitchen sink and feel the brush of Spirit against the backs of their necks, and know they have been visited. And still others will form a circle of light with those they love, with those who remain, summoning the presence of the dead through stories and laughter and the minutiae of the everyday, where most of life is lived and where so much of the dead remain, hidden in plain sight.

Sometimes when I feel alone, or when fear threatens to cloud my inner vision, I think of Yolana, of the things she taught me, of all that she embodied, and what was affirmed in her presence. I think also of those Saturday nights around the table with my family, our pinkies touching, forming a circle, as if that brush of flesh against flesh were enough to keep us tethered to this world, as if that one candle were enough to illuminate the darkness. In many ways, it was. And it continues to remind me that in this world, with its very real pressures, and perilous dangers, and potholes of meaninglessness, and losses that threaten to crush the soul, there is more. There is the adventure of not knowing. There is the hope that life goes on. There is the possibility of tuning in, of listening, of putting one's ear to the ground and suddenly hearing the ancient song of the earth, the eternal vibration of the universe, and realizing that it emanates from the depths of our own souls, which emanate in turn from the heart of God.

22

THE ACCIDENT

MONTHS BEFORE I WAS diagnosed with breast cancer, I would daydream about what it would take to make a major change in my life. How could I get off the train, so to speak? How could I get out of the rut and break the patterns in which I'd felt myself so entrenched lately? Driving along, I sometimes imagined having a car accident—nothing that would permanently disfigure or impair me, just something that would give me reason enough to slow down and stop taking care of everybody else.

Then the call came. I was sitting in the parking lot of the deli where I pick up my son every day from school. It was easier than negotiating the long line of cars that assembled for the smaller children. My son was in fifth grade and could easily walk down the hill from school and through the little patch of woods that brought him to the deli's parking lot. It was not a well-kept secret; many other children and moms had the same arrangement. The added benefit for my son was that he could usually talk me out of a couple dollars for an after-school snack at the deli.

So there I was, sitting in my car on a sunny April afternoon when my cell phone rang. My husband had gotten home early and called to tell me that there was a message from the breast surgeon's office. It was six days after a core biopsy had been performed. During those six days, I had not been obsessing over the results. Maybe somewhere in my subconscious I knew what the news would be, and just wasn't prepared to deal with it; but consciously, I did a very good job of convincing myself that I had nothing to worry about. I had had two fine-needle biopsies seven years before, which turned out to be benign, and I was banking on that same news.

The surgeon was not available when I returned her call, so I was turned over to a physician's assistant. She hesitated slightly when I told her my name, then asked me to hold while she went to retrieve my file from the doctor's desk. "Your biopsy came back positive for cancer," she told me. *What? What?* I heard her words, but someone had suddenly cut the cable on the elevator and I was plummeting down several hundred stories very quickly. The scene outside my window became blurred and surreal. I was vaguely aware of the fact that I still had my seat belt fastened—as if this would somehow protect me from the accident that was happening right now, in my car, not in my fantasy daydream.

"Oh my God," I think I said. "Really? Are you sure?"

"Yes . . . um . . . the doctor will want to talk to you tomorrow," answered the assistant.

"I think she left her cell number on my machine at home," I said. "I'll try to reach her right away."

"I'm sorry," stuttered the woman awkwardly. She sounded about twenty-five years old. I pictured her hanging up the phone and going on with her life. But mine had just come crashing to a halt.

As I closed my phone, there was a tap on my window. I looked up, somewhat disoriented, to see my good friend Jackie standing there. "Hey," she said, as I rolled down the window. "I've been thinking about you. How're you doing?"

"I just hung up from the surgeon's office," I stammered. "The biopsy came back positive for cancer."

"Oh shit," she said, taking my hand. "I'm so sorry. Shit."

"I know," I said, holding her gaze as my eyes started to fill.

Just then, my son appeared next to Jackie. "Hi, Mom! Can I have some money for the deli?"

"Sure, honey," I said, handing him a fistful of money. "Here you go. Take your time."

Looking again at Jackie, I tried to steady myself. Her hand on mine seemed to be the only thing keeping me from falling off the cliff along with my car.

"Listen," she said intently. "Call me, okay?"

"I will. I'll call as soon as I speak with the surgeon."

My son returned with his snack. We drove home. I asked him about his day, even though I was simultaneously hurtling through space at a nauseating velocity. His enthusiastic chatter and animated stories of dodgeball at recess and dissection in science filled the car, each story a balloon, a bubble, a cushion squeezing out the possibility of free fall, of crashing to the ground as we drove.

When I got home, I told my husband the news—then called the surgeon on her cell phone. She was alarmingly nonchalant. She confirmed the diagnosis, telling me that it looked like a mass that was moderately well differentiated (whatever that meant), and that it had to come out. The terms she used sounded like a foreign language to me: invasive ductal carcinoma, sentinel node biopsy, in situ carcinoma, tubular, lobular . . . I could hear her voice, but the words wouldn't quite register.

"What do I do now?" I asked, playing the part of the calm and obedient Ohio girl.

"Well, you should be scheduled for surgery," she answered.

"When? Soon?" I asked, still not believing that this was really happening.

"As soon as possible," the doctor replied. "Like next week."

Before the reality of my cancer had even registered, I was scheduled for a lumpectomy six days later.

Over the next several weeks, I could almost hear the gears screeching and scraping as my life came, indeed, to a kind of halt. I went on sick leave from my job. My parents, and then my sisters, came to care for me during the two surgeries (a lumpectomy and then a reexcision two weeks later in a failed attempt to clear the margins). Friends brought meals and flowers; my husband helped get the kids to where they needed to be. My focus was suddenly on trying to make the best decisions I could, not for my patients or even my children but, oddly enough, for myself, for my survival.

A few days before the first surgery, I spent hours at the hospital undergoing preadmission testing: EKG, chest X-ray, blood work. I was alone, and felt alone, as I made my way through the unfamiliar corridors. *What must this be like for non-English-speaking people or immigrants?* I asked myself. It was hard enough for me to navigate the system, a native to the language and one who had worked in health care for ten years. I determined to say a prayer for those I passed and with whom I sat throughout the day.

My first stop was for the blood work and an EKG. I looked around at my comrades in the waiting room, tempted to ask, "What're you in for?" like one in a holding pen at the county jail, but I refrained. We were of all shapes and sizes, ages, sexes, and colors. We read magazines; we stared at our cell phones. Some of us talked to family members who had accompanied us. We occasionally eyed one another with detached curiosity. *Is this purgatory?* I wondered. *Or does it only hint of things to come? Will there be a waiting room on the Other Side, where we are held until our name is called; where we will be screened and diagnosed, sifted and separated, wheat from chaff, sheep from goats, good from bad? No,* I thought again. *No, this is all we will know of purgatory and of hell. This here and now. This separating we do among ourselves—the walls we construct, the judgment we wield, the fear that grips us, the sorrow that hardens the heart—this self-inflicted pain is what keeps us from experiencing heaven, right here on earth. If the kingdom of God is within, as Jesus once said, then most of us need to do some interior housecleaning to find it.*

The sound of my name being called startles me. I jump up

awkwardly, as if someone else will claim to be me if I don't respond fast enough. An elderly Hispanic woman smiles sympathetically. *Poor little idiot,* she must be thinking. I am led to a small closet of a room and instructed to strip from the waist up. A green hospital gown is at the ready. Lovely. The one-size-fits-all dimension of it makes me feel vaguely anonymous and yet strangely connected to my cell mates in the waiting room. *We will all wear this gown,* I muse. Mostly, I feel naked and vulnerable as I wrap the thin cotton around my bare chest.

I cross the hall to the room where the EKG and blood work will be done and sit on the examining table, hugging my body tightly, feet dangling like a child's. A technician enters the room. She says hello without looking at me, in a voice that is neither friendly nor rude; if anything, it sounds merely indifferent. This does not bother me. I am so relieved that she is a woman, that I will not have to bare my chest to a man, that I exhale with gratitude. For a few minutes, I observe her as she stands reading the medical orders; her back is to me, curled over a small desk, one hand on her hip. Without turning around, she pauses to stretch, first her arms, then her neck. She bends it from side to side, then rotates her head slowly, like one in need of a good massage.

"Are you okay?" I ask.

"Yes, yes," she answers in a lovely Jamaican accent, sounding slightly startled to find me still there. Or maybe she is merely surprised by my question. "I just need to stretch every now and then."

"It must be hard working down here all day in this windowless room," I offer, looking around at her small office.

She turns and faces me, meeting my gaze for the first time. Her eyes are guarded, but warmth seeps around the edges. "It's not that," she says. "I don't mind the lack of windows. It's just that some of the patients bring such burdens. They lay them on you, you know? All of their stuff. And it can be so heavy. Some of the older patients still have ideas about . . ." She trails off without completing her sentence, but I have the feeling that what she is implying has something to do with racism, with the ways in which people treat her.

"I'm sorry," I say quietly. "I hope you have a way of breathing it all out, of decompressing before you go home."

"Well, I do!" she says, growing more animated. "I make sure that I take time to stretch when I am here; then, at the end of the day, I walk thirty blocks to the train station wearing my special hat—no matter what the weather is. Here, I'll show you."

She begins to rummage around in her bag for the hat. "Hmmm . . . where is it?" she says aloud. She opens some drawers; she checks her bag again. Still not finding it, she begins to approach what I would call controlled panic. *Find the hat!* I think frantically. *Find the damn hat!* This woman, after all, is about to stick a needle in my vein. I don't want her doing that under duress. Why had I even engaged her? Finally, she opens a cabinet, and there it is. "Aha!" we both exclaim. I don't know who is more relieved, she or I!

"Here it is!" she says triumphantly. It is a black cotton cap. "I know it doesn't look like much, but it helps me let this place go. I wear it as I walk those thirty blocks. There is a closer station, but I need that much time. When I get to the subway, I take the hat off. By the time I get on my train, I have let go of everyone and everything here, and I can go home unburdened."

"Sounds like a great meditation, a great system," I say, smiling.

When I extend my arm for her to draw my blood, we are breathing in unison. I usually hate getting blood taken, but this time, I am relaxed and peaceful. I barely feel the pinch of the needle. She instructs me to lie down for the EKG. As I do so, she asks casually what I am doing there. Opening my gown, I point to the deep purple bruise on my breast, evidence of the biopsy. "Umm," she says knowingly. True empathy needs few words. "You're going to be okay, sweetheart," she says softly in her musical voice. I shake my head, and tears begin to spill down my cheeks, pooling in my ears as I lie there. "No, I'm not," I choke. "I have breast cancer."

"Okay, darlin'. Easy now. Do you trust your surgeon?"

I nod.

"Well then, that's all you need to know. It's the most important thing. You have to trust your surgeon. You have to let go and let her do her work. She's going to get it all out of there and you are going to be fine. Okay?"

"Okay," I whisper. But what I am really thinking is *I trust you. And if you say it is so, I will try to believe it.*

It takes me a minute or two to slow the spasms of my breath so that she can get a proper EKG. When the test is completed, I sit up, refastening my gown. My technician's name is Bernadette. As she turns away to make a note, I say shyly to her back: "Make sure you stretch after I leave, Bernadette. I don't want you carrying my burdens."

"Oh no!" she says, spinning around and tossing back her head with a laugh. She faces me, placing her hands on my arms. She is smiling, radiating wisdom and love. "You are light, darlin'," she says. "Some people are heavy, but you are light." Then she enfolds me in a mother's embrace, holding me for a second against the warm expanse of her body. "You're gonna be okay, you hear me?"

I nod again. A few more tears spill but this time they are tears of gratitude. It is hard to leave her, but I do, changing back into my clothes and making my way to another part of the hospital for the next test. Only gradually do I realize that I am beginning to pull out of the ditch into which my car, my spirit had plunged. Bernadette helped me to get a wheel or two on dry land, where there is traction enough to inch forward. Compassion does this. It does not fix or cure, but it makes the way less perilous, less daunting. And so, with her kindness and her voice and her embrace, Bernadette sent me on my way—another thirty blocks and maybe I'll be free.

23

BODY AND SPIRIT

IT WAS TIME FOR the chest X-ray.

The last time I'd had a chest X-ray was years ago in my old doctor's office. He was an attractive, kindly man who had been an Army doctor during the Korean War. Articles to that effect decorated his heavy wooden desk in frames and under glass. He believed a good shot of penicillin in the bum would cure just about anything; and a chest X-ray was the best way to tell if you had a bad cold or pneumonia. A lot of the time, he was right—but my friends used to tease me about the frequency with which I dropped my pants or exposed my breasts in his office. They said it was not normal. A chest X-ray at his office would entail baring my breasts and having him take the pictures. It was always horrifying to me, but I would comply, telling myself that he was, after all, a doctor.

This was going through my mind as I waited to be called for the X-ray after leaving Bernadette, my EKG technician, in the belly of the hospital. "Please let it be another woman. Please let it be another woman," I found myself chanting silently like a mantra. Just then, a lovely Hispanic woman wearing a white lab coat and carrying a clipboard appeared. Her dark hair was smoothed back in a ponytail, her posture perfect, her manner poised. *Yes!* I thought with relief. But, strangely, the name she called did not resemble mine in the least. *This must be a mistake,* I argued to myself, because I had already started getting up out of my chair. She called it again. Determined as I was, I could not contort it to sound even remotely close. As I sat back down, a pleasant-looking, white-haired man rose to his feet (after a nudge from his wife). I forced the envy back down my throat, ashamed . . . but just barely.

After another minute or two, a young, handsome African American man appeared. "Andrea Raynor," he called. I blinked, adjusting to this reality like one whose hiding place has been exposed in a sudden flick of the light switch. My knee-jerk reaction was *Please, God, don't let him be the one to do the X-rays!* He was outgoing, friendly, and energetic—and way too attractive for me to feel comfortable about being half naked in front of him. *Okay, Lord, here we go,* I mumbled in my head. *Very funny. I get the joke. Learn to accept myself.* When you get the opposite of what you pray for, there's often a lesson buried in plain sight.

My smiling technician led me like a stable pony to the room with the X-ray machine. There was no sense in fighting it. *Just remember, you will never see this man again,* I said to my-self, as if that would spare me the horror and embarrassment to come. I just could not get used to baring my breasts all the time to strangers. It brought up all my insecurities and feelings about my breasts. Pointing to a small closet, he instructed me, per usual, to strip from the waist up and to put the gown on— opened to the back.

"To the back?" I asked with surprise.

"Yep, that's right," he answered cheerfully. "To the back."

I felt a rush of relief. To the back. Could this mean that I would not be exposing my breasts? I mean, how could I if it was opened to the back, right? I put on the gown and stepped shyly out of the changing room.

"Okay then," he said breezily, clearly trying to put me at ease. "Let's get started."

He gently positioned me with my chest pressed against a panel. "Is this it?" I asked, surprised. "Does the X-ray come through this panel?"

"Oh no." He smiled, looking at me kindly, as one does with all simpletons. "The X-ray is taken through your back. See there," he said, pointing toward the wall behind me. "That is where it comes from. Just try to hold really still so I can get a good picture, okay?"

If he had asked me to stand there and recite the Pledge of Allegiance, I would have done so gladly. I became the model of stillness, a regular Zen master. My gratitude for having gotten a reprieve from my self-hatred, or at least my self-conscious-ness, outweighed the shame at having felt this in the first place. *Must work on this,* I thought, making a mental note and flinging it to the back of my brain.

It took only a few painless minutes to do the X-rays. When they were done, my technician appeared, like the Great Oz, from behind the wall—a wall that protects him from daily exposure to radiation, a hazard of his job. "Want to see what we've got?" he asked with an easy smile. "Let's make sure we have a clear picture."

"Okay." I smiled back. He turned on a screen, and there, in an instant, was a picture of what lies, every day, every minute, every pulsing second beneath the surface of my skin. I looked at it—at me—in wonder. The technician began pointing out the various parts of my body, my ribs and clavicles, and the pear-shaped outline of my heart. He was like a proud father—adoring and energetic. He seemed genuinely excited to share his knowledge, not caring whether I already knew the information or not. That wasn't important. The point was that *he* knew, and what he knew was more than anatomy. His enthusiasm and awe gave the impression that he was letting me in on a great secret, namely that the body is a magnificent thing, a vessel of mystery.

Many thoughts passed through my mind as I stood there looking at the frame that holds me together. I thought of the bodies, broken yet beautiful, that I had seen at Ground Zero. I thought of the Spirit of Life, which swirls and pulsates invisibly through these bones and tissues, through the organs and cavities, and the blood that circulates in ever-constant rivers through our veins. I beheld myself, as if from a short distance, like a painter who steps back to consider her work. The symmetry of my lungs, the slight curve at the base of my spine, the shadow of my heart resting like a mysterious sea creature in a cave—I observed all of this with quiet reverence. And then I felt a well of love and care begin to surface for my little self. It was almost as if I was standing outside of myself, outside of this particular life, and feeling tender and maternal toward the self that I now embody.

Whoever lives in that little frame can't be all bad, I thought. I wanted to tuck myself under my arm, to shield myself, and to take me straight home! This is the only body I have to live in. This delicate collection of tissue and bone. I am the only me there will ever be. This life is the only one I can know for sure. There is no guarantee about the future; there is only here and now. How do I want to live?

How? Tenderly. Respectfully. Aware of the finite nature of our existence. Open to mystery, to the unexpected ways in which the Divine comes to us. I want to live with ears open so that I can hear others calling me. I want to live with some semblance of forgiveness toward the self that continues to stumble and fall. Because, somewhere, buried under the myriad day-to-days of our existence, buried beneath our fear and our insecurities, hidden under the surface of our skin, is the pulsating force of Life, ancient, unknowable, mysterious, and constant.

If I could put my ear to my own heart, like one listening for the ocean in a shell, what would I hear? Would I hear the voice of God? Would the drumbeat of my heart make me turn my horse toward home? Like one straining to make out the sound of words carried on the wind, I could only grasp fragments of meaning: Honor the Soul that lives in the body, honor your own body and those of others; the intricacies of the body point toward Mystery. And, finally: There is no separation between the physical and the spiritual—there is only and always the pulse of Life, swirling, moving, echoing, invisible, infusing all that is with something beyond our comprehension.

Listening to the whoosh and whisper of blood through the heart, of oxygen through the lungs may be the first step toward finding our way Home. And what is Home? Is it a feeling? Is it a sense of belonging? A safe haven? Looking at my X-ray, I began to understand that Home is rooted in a clear sense of who I am, both as a spirit and as a body. We live in these bodies, but few of us know who we are. The physical experience commands our attention—feed me, keep me warm, let me rest—but the Spiritual Self is the North Star by which we chart our course. The way will always be obscured if we fail to honor the Spirit within.

Perhaps this is why I always felt rising from the broken remains at Ground Zero was, strangely enough, a stubborn affirmation of life. The bones and tissues through which life had pulsed gave quiet witness to the uniqueness of each person who perished. DNA evidence meant finding an individual, connecting to a life, like a needle weaving in and out of fabric knit from the beginning of time. "Listen!" the bodies seem to say. "Listen to the voices which rise from these ashes. Listen to the Voice, still and small, within yourself. Listen, and you will hear that nothing can alter the inherent beauty of life." Each of us must look within to discover the beauty that is uniquely ours; and, discovering it, we must seek to honor it by becoming who we were created to be.

Looking at my X-ray, I began to grasp how little I know of myself, how little I understand. Looking at my X-ray, I began to hear a voice whispering, "Go within. Go within . . . and discover who you are."

24

FOR JEANETTE

Now I know I have a heart, because it's breaking.
—TIN WOODSMAN IN *The Wizard of Oz*

IN MY OPEN HANDS, I held my fear, that which symbolized the road ahead, with its unavoidable pain, and with its certain promise to pierce me, like an expert marksman, for life. In my hands was my wet ponytail, now limp and lifeless, severed just seconds ago from the nape of my neck. Chemo makes no empty threats—so I struck first, cutting my hair before it fell in fourteen-inch clumps around my shoulders, my lap, my pillow.

So this is it? I wondered. *This is what I feared, what I was so attached to? This is what I thought was me? This small, wet snake of hair, disarmed now in my palm?*

I observed it, I touched it; then I looked up at the face staring back at me in the mirror. Oddly enough, it was smiling.

I am free, I thought. *I am free from the attachment to this idea of myself. Free from the power I give this hair.*

Raising my eyes, I met the gentle gaze of my friend and hairdresser, Charles. His hands were resting on my shoulders. "I've been waiting twenty years to cut this hair," he said with a laugh. "Now we're going to have some fun."

I smiled, trusting implicitly in his expertise, his skill, and his understanding of who I am, my personality and my current struggle to come to terms with this breast cancer and the treatment which would soon make me bald. Crazy as it may sound, the prospect of losing my hair terrified me more than the possibility of nausea, of damaging my healthy organs, or of IVs piercing my veins on a regular basis. No matter how temporary I knew it would be, losing my hair signified losing an essential part of my identity as a woman and, even more, as a (relatively) young, vital, attractive woman. It was bad enough that my left breast had been carved to an odd and, in my eyes, disfigured proportion. That was my private pain. But who would I be under a scarf or a wig? I felt shackled by the image, and by the prospect of being unable to move freely about in the world, especially in this summer world of pools and convertibles, bikes and breezes. Cutting my hair was the only thing I could think of to help me prepare for this journey. I needed to let go—even if it was slowly.

Shutting my eyes, I saw the face of Jeanette. Jeanette, a beautiful twenty-two-year-old college student with leukemia whom I had met over ten years ago, just after I had begun working at hospice. Her doctor had called the office explaining to our administrator that, although Jeanette was not ready for hospice services yet, she was in need of spiritual support. She was a Catholic who had not found comfort in the visits by her priest or by the rabbi associated with her hospital. She was searching for meaning and comfort and for something to hold on to as she suffered through more treatments, more disappointments, and the roller coaster of hope and despair, fight and acceptance.

I was given permission to offer spiritual care to Jeanette despite the fact that she was not on the program. This was a rare but compassionate exception made by the powers that be. I remember being slightly nervous as I drove to the apartment she shared with her mother. Everything about this case seemed unusual. For one thing, unlike most of my hospice patients, there was still the strong possibility of effective treatment, if not cure, for Jeanette; and for another, I had not yet encountered such a young person. Not only was Jeanette hoping to get better, but she was determined to explore the existential nature of her suffering and to gain some measure of spiritual strength to help her in her struggle. Her one goal, she told me, was to graduate from college, to cross that stage, smiling and filled with a sense of accomplishment. This didn't seem to be asking too much.

As I drove, I tried to breathe and to clear my mind of any preconceived notions of what this young woman might need—from me, from God, from religious tradition. I wondered if she was looking for cure through prayer, or was perhaps expecting answers to her questions. What if I could offer no balm for her anguish, proving as disappointing as my anonymous colleagues the priest and the rabbi? I dreaded the idea of failing her, yet I knew that there was no rehearsing for a situation like this. *Just show up,* I reminded myself. *Show up and listen.* The reality was that I had no solid information about her medical status, information that might inform whether I should be guiding her toward accepting her disease or encouraging her to fight it. As always, the journey would be together, and the patient would have to be driving.

When the door opened to Jeanette's apartment and our eyes met, there was a ripple of energy. Energy, light, karma, love, whatever one might want to call it, boom, it was there. We smiled shyly, making our introductions, the momentary awkwardness quickly replaced by the powerful awareness of this sudden connection. She was at once my little sister, my teacher, my friend. I'm not sure what I was in that instant to her, but I think it was something close to a lifeboat, a safe place to rest and to cry, to wonder and to contemplate mystery. She invited me in, and we began our friendship curled on either end of a comfy, overstuffed couch, basking in the lovely light of a May afternoon.

This was Jeanette. She was a petite five foot one, with huge brown eyes that radiated intelligence and laughter, and too much wisdom, and the desperate hope of a child. Her smile was quick and easy, electrifying her face and sending light to her eyes. She wore a navy bandanna, evidence of the effects of her chemotherapy, but she wore it with the natural radiance of a college student, not a cancer patient. She was beautiful and smart and funny, and she seemed impossibly vibrant. Still, I had the strange sense that she was trapped in that apartment, like one falsely imprisoned, like one waiting to be set free.

Oh, God, don't let this child die, I thought as I sat down with her. *Please, God, not her.*

And so we began with hope: hope against hope against hope against hope. We hoped because it was the only reasonable thing to do. We hoped because it was still a realistic possibility that Jeanette might be eligible for a bone marrow transplant that could save her life. We hoped, and we talked, and I listened and offered what support I could. In the ensuing visits, we shared our ideas about God and prayer, and the possibility of healing. We explored what death might be like, what life after death might look like, and whether there was any interface between the worlds of spirit and earth. On a less metaphysical level, Jeanette shared her concern for her mom, a single mother, as well as her despair over wanting to be a normal college kid. When she was tired, I led her through guided meditations to relax and restore her, but mostly I just kept showing up.

During her last hospitalization, Jeanette was handed the disappointing news that she was not in fact eligible for the bone marrow transplant on which she was hanging her last hopes. This meant that nothing more could be done for her besides comfort care, and that her time was indeed limited. We sat together in the darkening light of her room as the sun began to set. It was quiet, except for the muted voices of evening nurses going about their work in the hall. Jeanette held my hand but turned her face away, tears falling in silent rivers down her perfect olive cheeks.

"I'm so tired, Andie. Tired of fighting. Tired of hoping. I don't want any more treatments. I don't want any more needles or blood work. I just want to go home."

"We'll get you home, Jeanette. You don't have to do anything you don't want to do," I said softly as something broke in my chest. Was it hope? Faith? Belief in a God who gives a damn? I wasn't sure, but I felt the shift. For all of our spiritual explorations, I had still been hoping, too.

"I don't want to go back to my apartment," she said quietly. "I want to go with my mom down to Atlanta to be with my sister and nieces. I want us all to be together."

Her voice was steady and had the conviction of one who was in charge of her destiny. I could feel her moving now. As the night continued its slow decent, Jeanette was gathering strength, gathering momentum. I could see it in her face. She was moving away from this world of doctors and nurses, of hospitals and of last hopes. She was moving away from goals that had anything to do with the future. She was watching one road evaporate like a mirage in front of her—a road that had included getting well, graduating from college, and moving on with her life—and, instead, stood like a warrior as a new road materialized. This road, while rugged and wild, would lead her home at last.

That was the last time I saw Jeanette. She did make it down to Atlanta to be with her sister and her family—Jeanette's physician made sure of that—and she signed on to a hospice program there. When I spoke with her by phone, the ring in her voice startled me. "Oh, Andie!" She laughed. "I am so happy. I have my sister and my nieces and my mom (and the dog is on the bed right now—I wish you could see him), and there are the most beautiful flowers in the garden. It is so perfect. I could not be happier."

I told her how glad I was for her. We both said we missed

each other. Jeanette gushed about how much our talks had meant to her, although, for the life of me, I could not quite believe how they had been of much help. I spoke to her mom and her sister, who promised to keep me informed of her status. Then I hung up the phone, struck dumb with awe. Jeanette's spirit humbled me. Clearly, she had accepted that she was going to die . . . but that ring in her voice, that laughter like water, confirmed without a doubt that she was happy, truly and deeply happy and at peace. A voice within her had said: "Find home. Go there. Don't stop until you get there; and when you arrive, drink it in, celebrate, live."

Jeanette died a few weeks later in her mother's arms, peacefully, serenely. I officiated at her memorial service at the college from which she had hoped to graduate. Several hundred of her classmates attended. Those who spoke bore witness to the remarkable spirit that had been their friend Jeanette, each one offering a different facet of her diamond presence. I stood at the podium still searching for the flash of those eyes, unable to believe that she was gone. It has taken me many years to integrate this reality into my psyche.

When the rest of my hair is gone, when this stylish new cut falls in tangled clumps about my shoulders, I will wear a bandanna and think of Jeanette. I will think of her courage. I will think of her pain. I will think of the way in which she carved her destiny from the rocky precipice upon which she was forced to stand. And maybe, if I have an ounce of her strength, that which is required to honor her, I will begin to carve my road, and go home by another way.

25

THE BRAVE TEST

I T HAD BEEN A difficult day. Starting with my oncology consultation at New York-Presbyterian, followed by navigating the medical maze at Memorial Sloan-Kettering with my friend Betty, I was exhausted and terrified. When the doctor at Sloan matter-of-factly informed me of his treatment plan, a plan (like all the others) that would involve months of chemotherapy resulting in the loss of my hair, the probable onset of early menopause, and the burning of my veins from infusions, I could not stem the tears that began to flow. He pointedly reminded me that, unlike my work with hospice, he was aiming for total cure, not palliation. I steadied my gaze and reminded him that, unlike his work, hospice acknowledges the suffering of the whole person, not just the physical. While I appreciated his interest in saving my life, I suggested that there might be a place for pastoral care in his office.

"Well, it's your decision," he said flatly, shrugging his

shoulders as a nurse handed me a tissue. As I reached for it, our eyes met, and I knew that she understood. Just because I wanted to live did not mean that this wasn't incredibly hard. I did not want to do chemo. I did *not* want to do chemo. I could hardly fathom that I had breast cancer, much less take in the full reality of what its treatment would entail. *I should be the one handing out tissues,* I thought, *not the one sitting in this chair.* That's who I *had* been for so many years as a hospice chaplain. But there's a big difference between witnessing a wreck and being the one in the car. Having worked with the dying for so many years, I never asked *why* this was happening to me—I had grappled with that question hundreds of times with countless patients—but it could not spare me the trauma or the terror of my own diagnosis.

I walked out of the consultation and found Betty in the large waiting room. She knew the place well. Betty was now being treated for metastases in her liver and lungs. She is one of the bravest people I know. Diagnosed with breast cancer in her thirties, she underwent a mastectomy followed by chemotherapy. In the eight months before her initial diagnosis, she lost her mother to cancer and suffered the end of her first marriage. Remarkably, two years later, she met a wonderful man, got married, and gave birth to a daughter on their first anniversary. She nursed her baby with the one breast she had, which is only part of the reason that she is one of my heroes. The other is that Betty has an extraordinary eye for beauty. She is a floral designer and decorator who has a unique ability to use colors, textures, and flowers to create atmosphere. This creativity is evident in her work and in the serenity of her home, where color and life quietly spill out the windows into her garden, and where one always feels an implicit trust in the sanity of the Universe.

I wasn't feeling too sane when I rejoined her in the waiting room. She had been waiting patiently for me for about three hours. In retrospect, I was too involved in my own drama to comprehend how little she must have wanted to be there (though she would argue with me about that). Collapsing in a chair, I could not stop crying as I told her of my consultation with the doctor who also happened to be her oncologist. Yes, he was brilliant, yes, he was straightforward, but I was still in shock.

I looked around the room and saw a woman, tall, smiling, thirtyish, wearing jeans and a baseball cap. She was casually leaning against a wall talking to a doctor in a white coat. Her face was glowing, but it was clear that her hat covered what was a completely bald head. *I don't want to be her,* I thought with a shudder. *I don't want to smile and act like it's all okay.* My projections and my fear made me feel ashamed in the face of her radiant smile.

Betty and I left the building and began making our way along the busy city sidewalk. My tears continued to flow as we walked. Suddenly, she took my hand like a child's and pulled me into a patisserie. "Come. We need chocolate." We plopped down at a lovely wooden table beneath a skylight where the afternoon sun was streaming in. There were green plants and light, and the muted sound of people chatting, and the smell of espresso. We split a decadent chocolate brownie, had some coffee, and breathed. I was slumped in my chair, shaking my head and apologizing for being such a coward, especially in front of her—she who had already endured so much. She squeezed my hand from across the table and said, "You *will* get through this." It was as much a command as a reassurance. I met her eyes, the color of the sea, of tides and waves, of storms and undertows, of life and time, and all we cannot know. I met her eyes, took a deep breath, and said, "Okay." I understood that "getting through" did not necessarily mean being cured; it meant something deeper. It meant that somehow the soul would survive, that the spirit would prevail. Looking in her eyes, I understood that, in order to find my courage, I would have to shake hands with my fear.

Over the next few days, I thought about what it means to be brave. I thought of Betty. I remembered the courage of others I have known who have died, or who've faced tremendous obstacles. I remembered reading somewhere that courage is not the absence of fear. I was afraid, and I had to start with that. But the more I accepted that I could not stop the direction in which the tide was taking me, the more strength I realized I had—not strength to change things but rather the ability to choose the way in which I would face this hideous reality. Feeling powerless was a road to despair; recognizing that the soul always has choices would be my way out.

I thought of being a child, of sometimes feeling vulnerable, of being afraid, of relying on my parents and others to order the world for me. And I remembered the dawning sense of my own innate power to act and to express myself in the world. While I was sitting with this, the following memory came to me.

It was 1968. My sister Jennie and I were sitting with our cousins and our oldest sister, Laurie, at the large oval table in the kitchen of my aunt and uncle's Ohio farmhouse. It seemed as safe a place as any to cast our lot with the big kids. What was the worst that could happen? There we were, sisters, cousins, left to our own devices as the adults worked the farm, out of sight, out of earshot, outside the realm of childhood rules. It could be a precarious place if you were a bottom feeder, meaning the youngest of the kids, which my sister Jennie and I were, because there was an unspoken agreement between us all, an understanding of hierarchy and risk. It went something like this: If you want to play with the big kids, you will not tell what goes on, you will not squeal or complain to the adults about what happens, you will accept the consequences of being allowed into the company of the older children, and you will not be given another chance should you decide to violate this privilege.

My aunt and uncle had two daughters, my first cousins Stevie and Shelley. Going to their house always afforded interesting experiences, like learning how to milk a cow, delighting in the baby piglets, trying to catch the feral kittens who lived in the barn, and riding behind my uncle's tractor. It also meant, for Jennie and me, the endless challenge of trying to get Laurie and our cousins to pay some attention to us. They were a few years older and usually could not be bothered with us—unless, of course, it meant having some fun at our expense. Thus began the tradition of the Brave Test.

The Brave Test belongs to my earliest memories of being with my sisters and cousins on the farm. It entailed the older girls putting Jennie and me through a series of scary and potentially dangerous tasks. It was a midwestern, kids' version of *Fear Factor*, circa the 1960s. These tests might include jumping off the chicken coop, reaching our hands beneath an unfriendly nesting chicken in search of an egg, being locked in the rabbit hutch (really not fun), or walking up the conveyor belt where the hay bales usually came down out of the barn. If we passed the tests, we were (theoretically) to be allowed to play with the big girls, or were at least permitted to tag along with them. Unfortunately, even if we were successful, by the time we had completed all of the tests, they would likely inform us that they were playing with us, and they had other things to do now. Or, as was often the case, we would emerge from the locked silo or darkened barn to find that they were gone, hidden now in the wilds of the farm.

Although Jennie and I were only a year apart and always had each other, we continued to want the company of the older girls. And so we found ourselves one afternoon at the kitchen table brokering a deal to play cards. The terms of the agreement were never negotiable; it was a take-it-or-leave-it kind of offer. If we wanted to play, we had to accept the consequences of losing. Conditioned by other forms of the Brave Test, we were undeterred. I remember my cousin Shelley smiling as she slowly shuffled the cards, her deep dimples flashing a warning that we should have seen. It was clear from the outset that the joke would be on us. The game was Spoons, and it was a game of speed and luck. Luck showed no bias; speed, unfortunately, would be our downfall. And they knew it.

I don't remember the exact rules of the game, but I do recall that the crucial part of it entailed grabbing a spoon from the middle of the table when someone played her hand. There was one less spoon than there were players, so the one who came up empty-handed would lose. Being twelve and fourteen to our seven and eight, the older girls knew that the loser would be either me or Jennie. "Here's the deal," Shelley said, sounding as friendly and nonchalant as possible. "You can play, but whoever loses has to eat some of my dad's Limburger cheese. No taking it back. No getting out of it."

"What if one of you loses?" I asked boldly.

"Same thing," she replied with a straight face. "Fair is fair."

"What's Limburger cheese?" asked Jennie, sounding concerned. Jennie, who ate only Velveeta. Jennie, who had the reputation in the family as a picky eater, whose only vegetable was corn, and who could have lived on peanut butter; she who used to slide peas and lima beans, carrots and broccoli, and anything else she didn't like onto my plate on a regular basis while our mother wasn't looking. She of delicate limbs and enormous brown eyes, a fairy child with dainty tastes. She had reason to be concerned.

My oldest cousin, Stevie, walked over to the refrigerator and pulled out a Tupperware container. She paused, dramatically, like a conjurer about to summon mystery. The room was silent, expectant. Then she opened it, and the most repulsive odor ever imagined escaped into the air like demon breath from the grave. "This," she said with a smirk, "is Limburger cheese."

The stakes were high, but we didn't care. Jennie and I were in heaven as the cards were dealt. We sat on our knees, elbows

pressed against the table, awash in the excitement of being included. We were not deterred by the unstifled glee of our sister
Laurie and cousin Shelley as the game progressed. We did not
catch the mirth that spilled from their eyes with each play. We
were focused. We were focused on staying in the game. It was
impossible for us to lose. We were doing it. We were keeping
up. We were . . . we were . . . we were reaching for that same
spoon, that same lone spoon, which somehow ended up in my
hand. For a moment we sat in silence. Four of us had spoons;
one of us did not. Jennie.

"Get the Limburger!" Laurie called triumphantly.

"No!" yelled Jennie.

"That was the agreement," Shelley said, laughing.

"No!"

"Better use a spoon so you don't hurt her," suggested Stevie, who was observing but not really participating in the punishment.

"Get her!" said Laurie, before the prisoner could make a
break for it.

As they grabbed Jennie, who struggled against them and
was starting to cry, it appeared for a moment that Stevie had
second thoughts and might intervene. "Wait!" she yelled above
the racket. *Was there hope?* I wondered. *Would she stop this
madness?* Then, with the calm authority of the oldest, she
spoke: "Better take her into the bathroom in case she pukes."

"Good idea!" they said, gleefully resuming their efforts and
dragging Jennie into the small bathroom directly off the kitchen.
I squeezed myself into the room with them as the struggle en-
sued. My hands were clutching the cool porcelain sink, Laurie

was between Jennie and me; Shelley was on the other side, blocking the door. I could see Jennie's face in the mirror, contorted, anguished. "Bring the cheese! Bring the cheese!" was the victory cry.

The smell appeared before the spoon. It was the most rancid stench I had ever experienced. It smelled of body odor and mold, and of all manner of foulness that my seven-year-old mind could imagine. Because it belonged to my uncle, I thought of his work boots, of the manure that caked the bottoms as he walked through the fields, of chicken droppings and pig slop and sweat, and the way his toes turned orange from the leather. I thought of the earthy smell of the damp mudroom, and of every reason why you were supposed to leave those work boots out there. My uncle was the sweetest, most mild-mannered soul you could ever meet, but he was also strong. Strong enough to work a farm. Strong enough to eat this Limburger cheese. This was no cheese for an eight-year-old girl, much less my fairy sister.

As Laurie and Shelley struggled to pin her arms and force her mouth open, I kept pleading, "Don't make her eat it. Don't make her eat it." This only made them laugh, because I still could not say my r's properly. "Hush up, Zsa Zsa!" they ordered with a laugh. That was their pet name for me when they wanted to tease me. They called me Zsa Zsa after Zsa Zsa Gabor because of my blond hair and the way I talked. Though it was innocuous, I assumed this was not a compliment since it came from them. "Me no Zsa Zsa," I used to protest when I was very small, "me Andie."

Now, the moment of truth was coming . . . the spoon was

coming. Jennie was crying but immobilized, her head forced toward the sink, just in case. I could not help her, blocked as I was by my older sister. I could only stand there, repeating my mantra, my protest, my shared despair. Jennie was thirteen months older than I was and had always been my security, my comfort in a strange and sometimes dangerous world. Her presence meant that I always had a friend, an extension of myself, someone who (in the realm of children) was in charge as the protector, the interpreter of life, the boss. Part of me looked upon her like a mother, but another saw her as impossibly delicate. I was aware that I was sturdier, more solidly built, more earthy than she was; and I was quite happy to play the page to her queen.

In some ways, it is no wonder, then, what happened when the spoon was thrust toward Jennie's face. In that instant, without thinking, without even knowing how it happened, my mouth closed in around the spoon. Interception. I had managed to thrust my round face in front of hers at the precise moment that the deadly delivery was being made. There was stunned silence. I swallowed. The only awareness I had of the cheese hitting the mark was the burning I felt in my eyes. I don't remember the taste. And I didn't puke. The five of us stood there blinking in the bathroom. Then came a cry of outrage. "Hey, that's not fair!" they protested. "That wasn't for you. Jennie's the one who lost. Stevie, get some more Limburger!"

Stevie examined the container of cheese thoughtfully. "Better not," she said, ever the practical one. "If you take more, Dad will notice that some is gone. You know how he likes this cheese—and he's the only one who eats it."

"Ah, you ruined it," they groaned, looking at me angrily.

But I wasn't looking at them, I was looking at Jennie. She was drying her eyes in a dignified, ladylike way, her long black eyelashes glistening. "Thanks, Andie," she said with a little sniffle. Then she took my hand, held up her head, and walked us, without a word, out of the bathroom, through the parlor with the player piano, and into the quiet of the living room, where we found some books that we'd read a dozen times before, and magazines with Breck girls, and puzzles with most of the pieces, and the deep hum of a connection that secretly knew what was brave.

POSTSCRIPT

ALMOST FORTY YEARS later, upon learning I had cancer, my cousin would write me:

Hello, sweet Andie,
This is your cousin Shelley checking in to let you know
my thoughts and prayers are with you. I hope you can feel
the amount of love, emotion, and positive energy that are
being sent out to you from Cincinnati. Who can know
why a beautiful person, both inside and out, is diagnosed
with this damn disease? It seems incredibly unfair. How-
ever, I believe that—just like eating the horrible tasting
Limburger cheese your evil cousin forced upon you when
you were a cute little girl, this nasty experience will also
pass and become part of your distant past . . . The bad
stuff will be over quickly and your busy life of mothering
and ministering will be at high speed.

I just wanted you to know my heart is with you. We all love you, Andie. From this point on, I can say without hesitation you have passed your Brave Test. No more jumping off of chicken houses, etc. You are officially the bravest of us all!

Much love,
Shelley

26

THE STRAW MAN

As I walked into the operating room at St. Luke's-Roosevelt in New York City for my second lumpectomy in two weeks, I was shaking. Nothing seemed to be going right. It was hard enough having to do another surgery so soon after the first one, hard enough to deal with the reality that my cancer was more extensive than originally thought, but now I was surrounded by what felt like the equivalent of flying monkeys. As the nurse yanked my hospital gown from my shoulders, exposing my breasts, she might as well have sneered, "You're not in Kansas anymore."

Surgery is never easy; but my experience at St. Luke's was surreal. The waiting area for patients going into ambulatory surgery had a bare, basementlike feel. It consisted of a narrow, windowless room crammed with a few hospital recliners where everyone awaited their turn for surgery. There was also a small locker room with a bathroom where patients first changed into their gowns. When I went in to change, the bathroom garbage can was stuffed with a bloody dressing. It was a stark advertisement of what I was about to go through—a vivid reminder that I would be feeling much different when I changed back into my clothing in a few hours.

Sitting down in one of the recliners, I glanced around. Another young woman was there, gowned and waiting nervously with her husband; an older woman had just vacated the chair in which I was now sitting. My husband and my two sisters were taking turns keeping me company, squeezing uncomfortably in and out of a space that didn't encourage visitors. We were like prisoners awaiting our trials. Was it death row or life row? That was the question. Adding to this feeling was the fact that, when it came your turn for surgery, you were not wheeled into the operating room on a gurney but rather were escorted in on foot—marched, as it were, by the unarmed guards otherwise known as nurses.

When the nurse came for me, I happened to be alone. I walked behind her into the brightly lit operating room and was told to hop up onto the table. I shivered a little, partly because the room was so cold and partly, of course, because I was nervous. Without so much as a word of greeting, much less an introduction (I would have settled for eye contact), one of the nurses pulled my hospital gown off my shoulders. When I told her how, before the first surgery, the nurse had just slipped my left arm out, keeping the rest of me covered, I got no response whatsoever. It was like being in a dream. I know that my mouth was moving, that I spoke, but everything continued around me as if I were not there, as if

I were an inanimate doll they were carelessly undressing.

The anesthesiologist, a young, nervous-looking fellow, arrived, proceeding to jab the IV into my left arm despite my protests. After a few unsuccessful attempts, he started in on my hand. As he poked at the vein, blood spurting, I told him that I had had lymph nodes taken out of that arm, that it was the surgical side, and that he should use the other one; but again, there was no response. The nurses continued chatting to each other, and the anesthesiologist dug till he found a vein. Meanwhile, I lay on my back, bare-chested, wrong arm outstretched and pierced, blinking at the bright light above my head.

As tears began to stream down the sides of my face, the surgeon came in and casually asked how I was doing. "I'm a little nervous," I whispered. The nurse who had pulled my gown off chimed in with irritation and a roll of her eyes. "Yeah, real nervous." Trying to ignore her, I pointed out that the anesthesiologist had put the IV in the wrong arm. The surgeon nodded, but then it was lights out for me. She later acknowledged the mistake but said there was nothing she could have done at that moment without upsetting me further. When I next opened my eyes, I was bound so tightly I could barely take a deep breath, and the recovery nurse was plying me with coffee because she said I needed to wake up and get going.

A week later the surgeon called to tell me that I still did not have clear margins; there was still evidence of cancer. I pressed the phone to my ear, clutched the kitchen table, and felt myself spinning. I was essentially missing the lower half of my breast after this last surgery, and yet the doctor was saying I needed more. She was recommending a mastectomy—*A mastectomy, for God's sake*—and all I could think was *She wants to cut my breast off. She wants to cut my breast off.* The light streaming into the kitchen from the May afternoon, which moments ago had looked lovely, now nauseated me; the world outside my window was a blur. Listening to the doctor speak, I half expected to see her fly past my window on a broomstick, the voice disembodied, the words not making sense to me. I was holding the phone, but I was falling through space like some cartoon character clutching a branch that had been sawed from the tree.

When I hung up the phone, the image of standing with my sister, Jennie, and my German grandmother in her small bathroom when I was about eight came to me. Her thin cotton housedress was unbuttoned to reveal an ugly concave scar where her large left breast had been. Her crystal blue eyes were watery red with tears, and through a smoker's rasp, she was saying to my sister and me, "Look what they've done to Grandma. Look what they've done." I remember focusing my eyes on the pretty glass doorknob, which suddenly seemed intricately fascinating. I remember my sister's unblinking gaze and the comfort of her presence, the nearness and familiarity of her perfect golden shoulder brushing mine, and her calm, almost clinical demeanor; and I can see my small hand slowly turning the doorknob, releasing us into what felt like cool, pure air.

My sister, not surprisingly, became a nurse—not because of my grandmother, although Jennie's ability to remain unfazed by medical procedures was certainly evident from an early age. She and I would later shake our heads and shudder a little as we remembered these moments with our grandmother, taking turns to exclaim, *"Ach!* Look what they've done!" Maybe we were being cruel, but I believe we were trying to offset the horror of that experience by acknowledging the narcissism and peculiarity of our father's stepmother. She had utterly disregarded the trauma her trauma could cause *us,* the images that would linger. "Look what they've done! Look what they've done! They've mutilated me. *Ach du lieber Gott im Himmel!"*

I stared in the mirror at my own disfigured breast. For the first time, I felt real sympathy for my grandmother. Yes, she had been inappropriate, but, truly, she had also been traumatized. Like someone suffering from post-traumatic stress, she was crying out to anyone who would listen, to anyone who would look, to help her make sense of things. She could not believe what had happened to her. Could *you*? she wanted to know. But people didn't talk freely of such things then. *Cancer* was a word that was whispered, as if saying it too loud would invoke its curse; reconstruction wasn't a routine option, and I seriously doubt counseling was ever offered. And so, like a wounded animal, she howled and clawed before any audience she could command, including her two small granddaughters, who had no choice but to bear pure, unencumbered witness.

While I was contemplating my next surgery, I underwent four months of chemotherapy, took long walks with my dogs, searched for another breast surgeon, and spoke with many women, both friends and acquaintances. I became used to the well-meaning, healthy women who would say to me, sometimes earnestly, sometimes flippantly, "If it were me, I would just cut them off." I would smile and nod, but inside I would be thinking, *You really have no idea what you would do until you get there.* Little did they know that the phrase "cut them off" would always be accompanied by that image of my grandmother crying in the bathroom.

I am not my breasts, I would tell myself, but it never helped much. I live in this body—this is how I know myself. My breasts, for better or worse, were not only part of my sexuality but were intrinsically connected to my sense of fertility, of youth, of being able to mother. The irrational horror that a mastectomy, especially a bilateral mastectomy, would mean that I could never nurse a baby again, that most likely my nipples would be removed, was terrifying to me. It was highly unlikely, at age forty-five, that I would ever be pregnant again, much less nurse a baby, yet I did not want this option literally cut from me. My breasts, my nipples, were symbols of my womanhood, my mothering, the nurturing I did, the nursing which lasted nearly two years for each of my children. I could not muster a cavalier attitude toward "lopping them off," even if it meant saving my life.

One thing was clear—I was not going back to St. Luke's, not going back to the nightmare of Dorothy's twister, which had brought me to the land of flying monkeys. Although I continued to experience a surreal sense of having being caught in a storm, blown into a foreign land by random circumstance, I knew I had to get my bearings and begin to make my way out of the wreckage, toward a plan I could live with. So I

picked myself up and began walking. I needed help, I needed friends; I needed to hear myself think.

During this time, I was corresponding via email with my friend Terry, who'd recently been diagnosed with bladder cancer. He had been grappling with the choice between two treatments: a less invasive but also potentially less effective bladder wash, or major surgery, which would entail removing his bladder and prostate, with all the complications and repercussions that implies. My impulse was to tell him to get out of Dodge, as if that would really solve anything. I felt terrified for him. I felt brokenhearted. Mostly I felt the enormity of what he was facing and wished there were some other way to ensure that he would be around for another fifty years. Big help I was. In the end, he made the decision, in his words, to "swing for the fences" and have the surgery. He pointed to his beautiful wife and six-year-old twins, and said he could not imagine facing them in a few years if the thing came back in full force without his having done everything he could to prevent it.

What I faced was profoundly less invasive and life-altering—another lumpectomy or a mastectomy—and I felt sheepish about tossing my situation into the dialogue. But I also trusted that friendship does not compare or disregard the suffering of the other; it listens with the heart and speaks from the same place. Terry reminded me that I am not my breasts or my hair but something closer to the light within. His decision to swing for the fences was made after carefully weighing what was most important to him—long-term survival, watching his kids grow up, loving his wife, "doing something spectacular at eighty"—and he encouraged me to do the same. His gentle suggestion that I not get hung up on the external felt far different from the casual lop-'em-off comments I'd received from some of my women friends. Clearly, he was coming from a place of compassion and shared pain. Facing potential impotence and incontinence, he dug down and discovered the eternal essence of his "sexy soul," his unique thusness, and he realized nothing—no scalpel, no doctor, no drugs—could touch that. Finally, he suggested that I, too, already knew all of this but that he was hoping to be "the straw" in my decision.

The straw. I thought about that for a long time. Thought about what he said, what he faced, and how he had come to his decision. I thought of what I knew of him. I have never seen him face to face, but I know him to be a man of adventure with a lust for life, a generous spirit, a gift for making good friends, and an ability to put his thoughts into startlingly clear writing. It was my husband who had first encountered him, through a motorcycle forum on the Internet. Quite often, he would call me in to read one of Terry's posts. They were always insightful, poetic, and witty, and sometimes they were spiritual. After learning about his diagnosis of cancer, I wrote him the old-fashioned way (via snail mail) to express my support and prayerful concern. We connected—and have been friends ever since.

I read and reread Terry's emails. I thought a lot. I walked along the beach and squinted at the horizon. I kept seeing that straw. Like Terry, I wanted to be here for my children, but I was scared. During these days, I would often stand bare-chested in front of the bathroom mirror contemplating my battered left breast. Sometimes, I would feel a deep and tender compassion for it, refusing to believe it could be harboring cells that were secretly waiting to kill me. Other times, I experienced a strange disconnect: Surely there must be some other way to help that poor girl in the mirror. Another lumpectomy would leave me with a permanently mutilated breast; a mastectomy, while offering an aesthetic improvement, would sever a piece of my body and my identity, a piece I could never get back. Other than that, I was just plain sad.

And so, I prayed for clarity and began to see the road ahead; I prayed for guidance and began to hear a voice whispering, "Live. Do what you can to live." The soothing lilt of my friends and loved ones mingled with this voice. "It's going to be okay," they hummed, they cooed, cradling me in a symphony of love. Terry's voice was in that chorus, too. He was somewhere ahead of me, dancing to his own song, forging his own path with courage and conviction. Perhaps it was his decisiveness that helped me make my own decision . . . or maybe he was, as he had suggested, that last straw. Either way, I had made my decision—there was no guarantee and there was no going back. There wasn't even certainty that what I was doing was the right thing. But I chose the path. Mastectomy, here I come.

Looking back, Terry was more than my straw, he was my Straw Man, my Scarecrow, in this adventure in Oz. I had plopped down from cyberspace, dizzy and bruised, before I even knew that I needed a friend to help me get home. When I found Terry along the way, I told him to *run;* he told me to hold steady. Now we are walking together. Like the Scarecrow, he is a true friend and companion on the journey. He instinctively knows what he needs—namely, the best chances of being around for as long as possible—and he is willing to keep me company as I continue to discover my own truth, my own path.

Perhaps we all inherently possess everything we will ever need in times of trial—the brains, the courage, the heart, the strength, the common sense, the faith, the trust. Perhaps all of these are in fact already ours. This doesn't mean that we have to go it alone, that we don't need anyone else. On the contrary, those whom we encounter—friends and companions, kind strangers, supportive communities—any of these might be the one to point out the ruby slippers that were always on our feet, the abiding Spirit that was ever there to guide us. As we accompany one another, we may each be the straw one day, providing that crucial breath of inspiration, that nudge toward clarity, but we can never be the final word. The other cannot do our work for us; we cannot ride the wizard's balloon, no matter how appealing that idea might be. Instead, we must discover for ourselves the truth of our lives, the meaning of our suffering, and the road that will lead us, one step at a time, toward our destiny, toward self-understanding, toward the awareness that each present moment is home.

27

THE BUZZ PARTY

AMIDST THE SOFT GLOW of Chinese patio lanterns, beneath a sky whose stars were hidden, we gathered. Seven women preparing to play Delilah. It was my Buzz Party, a party I had been anticipating since first learning I would lose my hair to chemo. I knew in my heart it was something that I would do. In the weeks leading up to this, I had talked about it frequently with my friend Brooke. Beautiful Brooke—a successful makeup artist, whose clients include movie stars and celebrities—is a native Californian, a blond bombshell, with stunning seafoam eyes and a sexy croak to her voice. She is glamorous, voluptuous, and self-deprecating (comically referring to herself as "Grandma"), and never fails to turns heads when she enters a room. One of the first times I saw her was years ago at a Brownie ice-skating party that both of our daughters attended. As she glided on the ice holding her daughter's hand, her blond hair billowing behind her, I remember thinking: *Someone that beautiful and that hip could not possibly be that nice.* Obviously I did not yet know her. For Brooke, while lusted after by men, is a woman's woman, a girl's girl. On her fortieth birthday, celebrated at a chic New York City club, she announced with genuine glee into the microphone: "To all my girlfriends here tonight—*you rock my world!*" Every day, I feel lucky to be counted among the rockers.

Brooke understood fully how traumatic it was going to be for me to lose my hair—she who specializes in beauty, who never judged my fear or the way in which I clung by my fingernails to that hair of mine, that particular image of myself. "I may not be as smart as you, Miss Harvard," she would laugh with mock offense, "but I can do your eyebrows and wash your wig, and I will help you through this. You might be HDS, but remember, I am FIT!" In the face of my beauty crisis, Harvard Divinity School was certainly no match for the Fashion Institute of Technology. In the face of my personal crisis, God was never as present as She was in my friends.

And so, like watching the darkening sky as storm clouds approached, I began to prepare. I circled the exterior, securing the windows, tying down loose ends, checking supplies . . . only I was the house. I made ready by first cutting my hair, the ten-inch ponytail now safely tucked in my dresser. (My highlights had made it unacceptable for donating.) Next, with Brooke's help, with the comfort of her presence and her professional eye, I bought a wig. Actually, many girlfriends and acquaintances bought the wig for me. When they learned how much a high-quality wig would cost (over three thousand dollars), Brooke and my friend Jackie had rallied a "wig fund." Whenever anyone asked them how I was or what they could do for me, they were told about the wig. "I mean, how many flowers and meals do you really need?" they would ask. Generously, without thinking, women I love and those I barely knew would whip out their checkbooks. Within about ten days, my friends had collected more than twenty-five hundred dollars—nearly the entire cost of my human-hair wig. The love that went into making that possible made it just a little easier for me to accept the reality of needing the wig in the first place.

In the weeks preceding my hair loss, I awoke each morning to the blank stare of that wig surveying me from its faceless form on the dresser. It was a bit eerie and unsettling really, like looking too closely at a future you'd rather avoid. "Do you really want that sitting out?" my husband asked me one day. I thought about that for a moment and realized the answer was yes. I left it there to get used to it and to make friends with it. I would brush it and occasionally put it on over my own hair. It always made me feel strange to do so, like I was dressing up for Halloween, and I would be relieved when I pulled it off my head. I seriously considered drawing a face on the wig form, but I was afraid it would come out monstrous and frightening looking, so I left it blank. It could be anybody that way. I could be anyone wearing it. I was everyone who has had to.

After my second chemo infusion, I knew the hair would be going. The doctors had told me, almost to the day, when to expect the start of the onslaught. They were compassionate but matter-of-fact. They had bigger fish to fry, like saving my life. Still, the reality was impossible for me to fathom. Maybe I would be different, I mused. Maybe I would be the one person who was invulnerable to this chemo, whose hair would wage a valiant against-all-odds struggle to stay put, there, atop the tower of my head, and that it would prevail. It had never let me down yet. Through the loose, long-haired years as a teen, through an unfortunate perm at twenty, through bleaches and highlights, and even the indefensible Linda McCartney look of the early eighties, my hair had always said a lot about who I was. Who would I be without it?

Then, a couple of things happened. First, I was talking on the phone with a dear friend, a nurse, who was tenderly offering me support and information. In the course of the conversation, she said, "And when you lose your eyebrows, there is a wonderful eyebrow clinic you can go to at . . ." To which I howled, *"What?* I'm going to lose my eyebrows, too?" This had not occurred to me. It was bad enough that I would lose my hair (atop my head and everywhere else), but my eyelashes and eyebrows as well? I burst into uncontrollable sobs, her soft Irish brogue barely audible on the other end of the phone. The storm was beginning to blow; shutters were rattling. Eventually I would be grateful for that information and for the compassion with which she offered it. But it had caught me by surprise, like a gust of wind that suddenly turns your umbrella inside out.

Right on cue, the first handfuls of hair began to escape. In the shower. In the brush. In my hands anytime I touched my head. I would be driving with the car window open and just pull out handfuls of hair, releasing it to the wind. My temples were beginning to recede. I was in freak-out mode. I put on a scarf, trying to channel Nicole Richie or Johnny Depp (it was, after all, the summer of another *Pirates of the Caribbean*), but it didn't work. There was a war going on. It was on my head and in my soul. My scalp became a map of terror. Hairs were everywhere, like refugees or prisoners of war who had no choice but to drop and surrender where they were. "Now what?" they seemed to say from my shoulders, from my car, from the kitchen floor.

I needed help, so I called in the troops. My best friend of twenty-five years, Katherine, was my lifeline. Her voice on the other end of the phone did more to steady me than any book I could read, any survivor story I could hear, any reassurance by the medical profession that "it would grow back." We had been through divinity school together, had studied together, played together, graduated together, lived together. We had suffered through romances, heartbreaks, boyfriends and husbands; we officiated at each other's weddings, were godmothers to each other's children. Since the advent of cell phones, we have talked at least once a day, every day. Sometimes, when I call her, I will begin keying in my code when her voice mail picks up, mistaking her voice for mine. She has been known to do the same thing. We refer to each other as "Best, Bestest, Beloved Best, et cetera," which makes my daughter laugh and my husband roll his eyes. Clearly, if anyone could understand my anguish, it would be her.

"Best," I stammered. "Help. I am Alice falling down the rabbit hole. I am tumbling through space. It's just so surreal. I mean, the surgeries are hard enough, but this? Do I have to *look* like I have cancer? Can't I just have it? Believe me, I get it! Why do I have to have cancer *and* look like a freak?"

"Oh, Bestest." Her voice came, warm and invisible, through the receiver, spilling into my ear, filling my lungs again with oxygen, resuscitating me. Like the Annunciation of Mary, life was entering through my ear. "Listen," she said, "do you want me to come down again? I'll be there in a heartbeat if you need me, you know that."

"No, it's okay. You were just here for my surgery. There's really nothing you can do. But hearing your voice helps more than you know."

"Just keep breathing, Andie. Call me every second—and call some of your girlfriends there. I'm so glad you have so many good women around you."

Katherine lives in Vermont, some five hours away from me, and she understood that, in addition to her, I would need the flesh-and-blood presence of my female friends. My husband did all he could to support me, to empathize with me, to give me space, and to mourn with me; but he came to understand that I needed the identification of other women.

One of the people I turned to was my friend Chris. Chris is a hospice social worker and a Zen practitioner. Her prematurely white hair and clear green eyes, along with her steady presence, always make me feel cool and calm. She mentholates my spirit, making me feel like I'm surrounded by snowcapped mountains or peering into the center of a crystalline glacier. She is a deep thinker, insightful and wise, and slightly spacey in the best way, and has a rich laugh that rumbles like an earthquake from somewhere below the surface.

I called, she came. We walked along a gravel path that separates the green town park from the sandy beach and the blue ocean beyond. It was a beautiful Saturday in July. Families were playing in the park, people were strolling lazily, children carried sand in buckets on the beach, the sound of someone's boom box floated on the breeze. We stopped to rest on a bench. I looked out at the water, I looked at my hands; I looked into her eyes, feeling miserable, pleading, having (one could say) a *moment*. "I don't want to be brave," I remember saying out of the blue, for she had not suggested anything of the sort. "I don't want to wear a scarf and big earrings and bright lipstick. I don't want to sport pink ribbons and 'walk for the cure.' I don't want to be Lance Armstrong. I don't want this *at all*!"

"You don't have to be anyone's hero," she said gently. "People can get their own Lance Armstrongs."

"Well, that's a relief," I responded rather petulantly. "Because I'd make a bad one."

I adjusted my bandanna, and a hank of hair escaped into the breeze, dispersing like so many strands of golden corn silk. We laughed, bitterly, mournfully, then walked some more, out of the park and across the street. We veered off on a dirt path that led us through a cool patch of trees, and along a salt marsh where tiny crabs scurried purposefully on the bank, going nowhere in particular, and wild ducks dunked their heads to get a better view of lunch.

I could see the roof of my house across the marsh grasses, which swayed in the breeze. The grasses were a vibrant green now. They would begin to turn gold by fall, slowly fading into a soft, pale brown by the winter. In the spring, new life would begin to overtake the dry stalks from the ground up, climbing toward the sky until they became a lush green. But this was the height of summer, and in summer, the marsh stretched its verdant fingertips lovingly to the sun, waving in gratitude to the source of life. It was a cycle whose beauty always spoke to me, and I tried to breathe it in, tried to feel that gratitude, that connection to my Source.

We came out through the old cemetery, with its graves that date back to the 1600s. It is a mystical place, though one that can easily be invisible because of its familiarity. Cars zoom past it every day, joggers barely look over as they run past with their earphones on. But at night, it begins to sing. If I walked past it in the dark when my children were little, they would cuddle into me, squeeze my hand, and whisper, "Look, Mom, there're your peeps. But we're not afraid . . . you *know* these guys." Somehow they thought that my being a hospice chaplain meant I knew *all* dead people.

Chris walked me to my house, leaving me with the marsh and the cemetery, with the families on the beach, and with permission to be upset.

The next day was Sunday. It was raining heavily now. Not precipitation but hair. It was raining hair. The storm was in full force. I took my dogs back to the park for a morning walk. Each step seemed to shake loose more hair, like leaves from a tree. It was summer in the park but autumn on my head, and I couldn't stop it, any more than you can stop the winter from coming. I finally accepted that it was foolish to try.

I leaned against a big rock in the center of the park, the dogs resting at my feet, and took a sip of coffee. It was a perfect summer morning, my favorite time of year. I breathed in the green of the grass, the dark, cool shadows cast by the trees, the sun spilling its diamond light onto the waters of the sound. Just as I began to take my first deep breath, a Park Nazi (otherwise known as a security guard) approached in a golf cart, telling me to leash my dogs. I looked around—there was not another soul in the park. "Just give me a minute," I pleaded quietly. "The dogs are right here by my feet—they're not going anywhere. I've got two leashes and one cup of coffee to juggle. Just let me catch my breath." "Well, all right," he grumbled reluctantly before zooming off in his cart.

I exhaled and decided to call Brooke. The time for the Buzz Party was at hand. As I pressed my ear to the phone, I was startled to find Park Nazi barreling toward me again. "Hey!" he called angrily. "I told you to put those dogs on the leash! You asked for a minute and I gave you one. Now you're making a phone call! Leash them or get out!"

I looked around the park, still populated only by squirrels and birds. I looked at the dogs sleeping by my feet. And I looked at the man glaring at me inexplicably from his cart. "What is your problem?" I asked, voice shaking. "There is no one else here. We aren't bothering anyone. Yes, I made a phone call. And do you know why? Because I have cancer and I'm losing my hair and I needed a moment to breathe, and I needed to call a friend. Can you understand that? Do you have nothing better to do than to harass me?"

"I'm just enforcing the rules," he said, squaring his shoulders and thrusting out his chin with forced bravado.

"Congratulations. That's exactly what the Nazis said," I shot back over my shoulder as I began to walk away. "Come on, boys," I said to the dogs. Satch, the English bulldog, and Rocco, the Brussels griffon, miraculously sprang to their feet upon my command. Normally, they would have looked at me lazily, reluctantly, pretending not to hear. But, for one shining moment, they were perfect. Even in my anguish and fury, I was secretly astounded by them, grateful to them, proud of them. I turned and walked with long strides away from the man and the cart and his rules and his stupidity and lack of compassion, tears streaming down my face, dogs trotting like champions at my heels; then I remembered that I still had Brooke on the phone. I had completely forgotten about her in the midst of the confrontation with the park man.

"Are you okay?" she asked when I returned the phone to my ear. "I could hear you talking to someone."

"No, not really," I cried. "It's just that awful man in the cart again. I mean, it's so *stupid*. There is *no one here,* and we weren't bothering anyone, and I just wanted to sit by that rock with the dogs, and my hair is falling out in handfuls . . ."

"Oh, honey, where are you now? I'll be there in two seconds."

"No, it's okay," I said miserably. "You don't have to come. Really. I'm just gonna walk."

"I'm coming," Brooke responded simply. "Where are you? On the boardwalk?"

"No, well, almost. I'll just sit here and wait."

I plopped down, cross-legged, eyes on the dogs, fingers in the grass, mindlessly pulling up blades, only half aware of the irony that the breeze was doing the same to my head. Within minutes, I felt an arm around me. It was Brooke, with her giant sunglasses, her pajama bottoms, and her hair in a pony-tail. Grandma to the rescue.

"Look at this," I said, pulling a handful of hair out of my head. "It's really happening." I shook my head, and hair blew away like fairy seeds from a dandelion carried on the breeze. But it was no use making a wish.

"Oh, baby, I'm so sorry," she cooed, pulling me toward her and rocking me gently. She stroked my head and came away with another clump of hair. "Oh, shoot!" she said, letting out an involuntary gasp. We both had to laugh, even though tears were spilling down my cheeks.

"It's time for the Buzz Party," I said resolutely. "I can't take this slow torture. I want to do it while I still have a choice."

"Okay, okay," she said. "Whatever you want. You want to do it tonight? You tell me who you want there, I'll do the rest. I'll get some food . . . we'll make it nice. Okay?"

And so it was decided. That night, a remarkable group of women assembled on my behalf. There was Brooke, of course, and my friend Jackie, a freelance writer and yoga buddy. There was Candace, a public relations consultant and free spirit (a friend from the dog park), and Betty, a floral designer who had battled breast cancer seventeen years ago. The night of the Buzz Party, she was awaiting news on a scan that would ulti-mately reveal metastases on her liver and lungs. Then there was Perrin. Shy and intellectual, she is a curator at the Metropoli-tan Museum of Art and had just completed her treatment for breast cancer a couple months earlier. To support me, she left her wig at home and bravely showed up in a bandanna. And, finally, there was Robin. Grounded and smart, she is an art di-

rector for *Newsweek,* the daughter of the former mayor of San
Francisco, Willie Brown, and the one who provided our
"buzzer." She probably had the most experience with it, having
kept her own hair closely cropped at one time in her life.

As we sat on the patio eating sushi and fruit salad, guaca-
mole and chips, sipping wine and sharing with one another,
there was a lovely energy among us. Some of the women didn't
know one another—for a few, I was the only connection—and
it was soothing, somehow, to hear them tell their stories. Soft
music was playing on the speakers outside, and occasionally
you could hear a car pass beyond the high fence that hid us,
like a mother hen, beneath the shelter of her wings. We were
nesting there, on that warm patio, in the twinkling glow. The
night air was full of expectation and purpose, though part of
me wished that the cup would just pass, so to speak. Wished
we could just give each other a little hug and go home.

Perhaps they sensed my creeping anxiety, or perhaps out of
love they simply became the sisters in charge. Either way, they
started to nudge me toward the business at hand. Before we
began, I read a couple poems from Rumi—then I told each
one of them why she was important to me, what she meant to
me, and what I admired about her. They teased me, of course,
about having to officiate at my own party. "Can't stop being
the minister, can you?" They laughed.

Then it was time.

Brooke led me to a high stool, then handed me a hairdresser's gown to put on. When I put it on backward, she pretended to scold me. "Okay, who's smart now? That's not a
clergy robe, dumb-dumb! Lucky for you, Miss FIT's in charge.

Give that here." We all laughed, nervously, gratefully, as she helped me with the gown. After a brief consultation with Robin, Brooke started buzzing my hair. The women took turns holding my hands and rubbing my head. Tears started streaming down my face, but I was calm inside, like a warrior priestess being prepared for battle. After a few minutes, Brooke said quietly, "I . . . I don't want to be the only one responsible for this." "Here, give it to me," Jackie responded. "I'll give it a shot." Jackie continued the process—then, when it came down to the closest part, Robin took over. I kept my eyes shut most of the time, squeezing the hands that held mine and envisioning sparrows and cardinals softening their nests with my hair in the morning.

Periodically, I would hear the warm coos of the women, encouraging me, doting on me: "Doesn't she look cute?" "You look very punk." "You look like a kid." "What a nicely shaped head you have." "Look at her beautiful face." "She looks like a Buddhist nun." When it was over, I ran my hand over my bare scalp and let out a little cry. Okay. It was done.

"Wow. You look beautiful," someone said.

"Hardly." I smiled, feeling naked and vulnerable.

"No, I'm serious. You do. You look just like you. It's still your face, your spirit."

I went inside to the bathroom to take a look, and promptly burst into tears. Somehow their words of reassurance had buoyed me into believing that I looked okay, beautiful even. But what I saw in the mirror devastated me. I took a deep breath and went back outside. When the women saw my face, they again rallied around me, wiping my tears and rubbing my back. To shift the mood, I showed them my wig. They oohed and aahed. A couple of them tried it on. Brooke ran inside— and came back out wearing a long, black one with shaggy bangs. It made her look very rock 'n' roll. "I have a couple of other cheapies," she said. "I think we should all get dressed up, wear our wigs, and just have some fun! We'll have lunch in town. You will, of course, look the best," she said, motioning to me, "since you have that beautiful human-hair one." We all laughed.

Then she popped open some champagne and we toasted ourselves. We toasted our courage, we toasted our friendships, we toasted the moon, which finally got around to showing its face. The night air fell softly on my head, anointing me with moonlight and cricket songs, with the hush of women's voices and the flicker of burning candles. I looked around at my Delilahs as we sat in a circle beneath the patio umbrella that we no longer needed. There, in that glow, I knew they had not cut my strength from me (as was the case with poor Samson) but had helped me find my power. And somewhere, beyond the patio and the fence and the lights, the ghost of Delilah, goddess of scissors, smiled. This time, she got it right.

28

AFTER

FTER THE CHEMO AND the surgeries, after every hair had fallen out, the last eyelash surrendered, after the shock had worn off about the fact that I had had cancer, then began the rebuilding. Perhaps I never doubted there would be an "after" because I could conceive of no other possibility. Even when we are presented with a life-threatening illness, our own mortality is nearly incomprehensible.

In the early days of my "after," before the final reconstructive surgery, I would sometimes catch my reflection in the bathroom mirror as I climbed out of the shower—and it would startle me. There, staring back, was someone/thing I barely recognized: a completely hairless creature with exposed, naked eyes, long, ropy arms, and a large orb protruding oddly from the left breast (courtesy of my skin expander). *Who is that?* I would wonder, with the same morbid curiosity with which one approaches all things freakish. I would pause to study the reflection, which bore a striking resemblance to some strange alien creature, and imagine myself emerging from a slimy pod. I didn't feel as sick as I looked—yet my appearance undeniably confirmed that what I had battled was no joke.

Running my hand over my scalp, I would think of the people (though they were few) who had questioned why losing my hair had been such a "big deal" to me. How could they understand what it was like to stand here, staring at the alien in the mirror? Who could know how difficult it was to begin every day with trying to decide what to put on my head, trying to draw eyebrows that didn't render me some scary version of Baby Jane, trying to figure out how to present myself to the world. *Why* was it so hard to lose my hair? Because I had lost a part of myself. I had lost a confidence and ease when I walked down the street, and the freedom not to think about how I looked. I had lost my sense of femininity and anonymity, feeling, instead, imprisoned by the evidence of my disease. My bald head meant wearing my cancer like a neon sign every time I walked down the street. It took away my privacy and made me feel like something had been done *to* me rather than *for* me. It was a double-edged sword representing the price I had paid for the chance to live. By most standards, it was a small price, but I hated when others made this point for me.

Compounding how I felt about myself was the way my lack of hair rendered me invisible as a woman. One might think that, while battling cancer, this would be a nonissue. But remember: denial, denial, denial. I had cancer, sure, but I still wanted to be *me,* and being *me* meant feeling basically good about myself as I moved about in the world. I wasn't nineteen anymore, but I still got the occasional smile or whistle from a passing stranger. And, as anyone over forty knows, you take what you can get. But bald me? Well, as they say in New York, fuhgeddaboudit!

This was strikingly obvious when I was in New York City one day with my friend Brooke. It was a few days after the Buzz Party, and we were going to pick up my wig. I had taken it back to the salon in preparation for the final fitting. Without hair, wigs fit quite differently and need to be adjusted. We were wearing breezy summer dresses, cute sandals, and fashionable sunglasses. I wore a pink scarf tied casually around my head and pretended to feel chic. As we walked briskly along the city blocks, I noticed the usual coterie of men looking and smiling at Brooke but barely glancing in my direction. Normally I would have teased her about this; normally I wouldn't have cared. But I was feeling anything but normal, and so what it did was scream "painful ugly reality" to pain-filled, freaked-out me. *It's all about the hair,* I thought bitterly. *I'm ugly without my hair.* I mentioned these feelings to Brooke, but she shrugged them off, trying to reassure me that I looked hip. "Come on, crazy girl," she laughed, gently taking my hand.

When we got to the wig shop, a high-end midtown establishment, the owner happened to be there. He showed us into one of the cubicles that afforded customers some privacy, sat me in a chair, and nodded approvingly at my borrowed Hermès scarf before sliding it off my head. I felt strange and vulnerable as he casually ran a hand over my bare scalp before going to retrieve the wig. Maybe bald heads invoke the same tactile curiosity as pregnant bellies—some people want to feel you, they want to run their hands over you, assuming you don't mind. I didn't know whether I minded or not. I didn't know what to feel. I was trying hard to detach from the curious creature in the mirror, she who had kidnapped my reflection. I could barely meet her gaze. Brooke came and stood close behind me, her hands on my shoulders, as we faced the mirror together. "You okay, sweetie?" she asked softly. "This is going to be good, you'll see." I took a deep breath and just tried to surrender. What else could I do?

Soon the owner reappeared like a suave party host, with a silky swish of hair in his hand. He promptly secured it to my head with the requisite double-sided tape, tape that bore the unfortunate label MEN'S GROOMING TAPE (how attractive). I let this go for the moment, gathered my strength, and looked in the mirror. To my surprise, the alien was gone, replaced by someone who looked a lot like me. Soft blond hair fell perfectly down my forehead, cheeks, and neck. It looked stunningly natural, and incredibly close to my own hair. I exhaled, surprised by how restored I felt. Brooke gasped with approval as she ran her hands through my new hair. "Look at you!" She laughed. "You look beautiful!"

"Do I look wiggy?" I asked tentatively.

"Not at all," she reassured. "Not at all." Then she dabbed a little makeup on my face in an attempt to bolster my spirits and my confidence, and we headed back out into the bustling July afternoon.

"Let's see what happens now," I said with an edge that revealed a mixture of sarcasm and uncertainty.

Sure enough, the smiles were more even as we walked. This time, we were just two women bouncing along the city street. I felt a little shaky in the wig, especially when the wind blew, but less self-conscious than I had in the scarf. At least it wasn't screaming "chemo girl." At the same time, I realized that I would have to make peace with this new reality, the reality that I was not the same person, that I would have to incorporate my new identity—as chemo girl, cancer woman, wig wearer—into the me I had known for forty-five years.

I am aware that this may sound like an embarrassing exercise in vanity. Perhaps it is. But the feeling of being victimized is still hard to shake. I would never have chosen to have short hair, much less no hair, but I had no choice. And it is the lack of choice coupled with one's self-image that deepens the psychic blow. I had relied on my hair in ways I had not even been conscious of. It said something about me, as all of our appearances say something about who we are. Sometimes I was hippie chick, sometimes practical mom, sometimes sexy woman, sometimes just natural me. But through all of these incarnations, I associated something of my feminine power with my hair. I am hard-pressed to think it is the same for men—and perhaps it is not the same for other women—but I know this was true for me.

In the same way, I never would have chosen to have a "boob job," but here I am with altered breasts. Some days, I feel like Mrs. Potato Head, the passive subject of someone else's experiment, someone who found hilarity in mixing up my parts. I feel no malice in it, just the danger of whimsy and chance. The problem is, I will have to wear the evidence of this cosmic game—there is no switching back, no reverting to the original model—and this is a challenge. But I am learning. "At least you're here," people say. "At least you've got your health." They are right, of course, and I do try to remember that. These words were hard for me to hear in the beginning of this journey because they often seemed to invalidate what I was feeling. Now, as I heal, I can accept the wisdom and the truth in them.

In some ways, it was my eleven-year-old son who first helped me find my strength, who gave me the proverbial Zen slap, and helped me to get a grip. We were sitting together in the car when I began to explain what chemotherapy was, why I needed it, and what it would do to and for me. As I tried to prepare him, saying that the medicine might make me look and act sick and that I would lose my hair, I began to cry. He was quiet for a moment—then he looked at me with his large hazel eyes and said in a strong, steady voice: "Well, Mom . . . would you rather die of cancer or be bald for a little while and be with me?" Squeezing his hand, I said, "Alex, I would be bald my whole life if I could be with you."

"Good." He nodded, in a that's-settled-then type of way. Then he squeezed me back and said tenderly and sweetly, "It *will* be only a little while . . . You'll still be my beautiful mom, even when you're bald. And I will always love you."

Now I don't feel beautiful, but I feel stronger. I am Mrs. Potato Head with a sense of humor. My parts have been exchanged and rearranged a couple of times. I joke that I have twenty-five-year-old boobs and a forty-six-year-old bum. My hair is growing back, but in a color and texture that are unrecognizable. I have outgrown the wig but still feel frumpy and unattractive without it—and I have yet to figure out how to manage the curls that have replaced my straight hair. It is difficult to talk to people about what this feels like without sounding like I am whining, or am not grateful for having my life and my health—which I am.

This is part of the "after." Learning how to be from this day forward. I am not the precancer me, and yet I am moving, each day, away from the epicenter of my trauma. As I step away, I am able to see more clearly all that I have to be grateful for—and it is gratitude that will ultimately heal and restore me. I'm not sure whether gratitude points the way toward wisdom, or wisdom leads toward gratitude, but I am certain that both are required in the journey toward wholeness, both will inspire compassion—toward myself and others.

One of the people for whom I am especially grateful is Dr. Barbara Ward, who became my new breast surgeon. When faced with the reality of needing a mastectomy, after the two disappointing (and traumatic) lumpectomies, I knew I could not go back to St. Luke's. My sister the nurse had been researching the idea of a "nipple-sparing" mastectomy and urged me to ask the new surgeon if this would be possible. Living just outside of New York City, I turned naturally to Memorial Sloan-Kettering. The surgeon with whom I consulted was compassionate, kind, and clearly quite brilliant—but he did not seem keen on the idea of sparing my nipple. His mission was simply to give me the best possible chance of avoiding a recurrence, ensuring the strongest warranty on my health. I appreciated this, but I also knew I had to consider the emotional factors that would inhibit or enhance my inner flame, my ability to overcome the trauma of this illness and the assault to my sense of self.

Several people had recommended that I consult with Dr. Ward at Greenwich Hospital in Connecticut. My initial bias that one had to go into New York City to receive good care vanished the moment I met her. She inspired complete confidence as a surgeon and was utterly present to my suffering. When I inquired about the nipple-sparing procedure, she didn't refuse it outright but thoughtfully considered whether I would be a candidate. Although she didn't promise me anything, she said she would begin by taking a close look at the reports from the first two surgeries. In that first consultation, she didn't give me a guarantee, but what she gave me was hope—and that was balm for my frightened spirit.

What could have been the road to more despair, more feelings of being mutilated, turned into the path of healing thanks to Dr. Ward. When she hugged me just before performing my surgery, I flushed with gratitude. It felt a long way from the terror of that second lumpectomy at St. Luke's. Dressed in her surgical gown, speaking gently and sincerely, Dr. Ward reiterated that she would try to spare the nipple but could not guarantee it. She carefully explained that if any cancer cells were found in the tissue just behind it, my nipple would have to go. Looking into her kind, intelligent eyes, I could accept this. Odd as it may sound, I was not without fear, but I was at peace.

I had always thought of my left breast as my nursing side, the side to which I had most naturally held my babies—to me,

to my heart, to the fount of nourishment my body was so able
to supply. I had, of course, nursed them on both sides, but the
left was where they would finish, where they would fall into
the blissful sleep of perfect contentment. I guess I finished
there, too, resting in the circle of love, gazing into the face of
my little Buddha, and being filled with the wonder and the
completion of our intimate universe.

If I had to lose my nipple to save my life, so be it. It was a
horrific prospect, but I could accept it. I could look at my children, at the shape of their mouths, their broad palates, the
strength of their upper lips, and trust my work was done. My
nipple had done its job, and I was grateful. This time, as the
anesthesiologist began his work, there were no tears. Instead,
something in the depths of me murmured, "Namaste. I bow to
my nipple, the manifestation of the Great Mother in me. Namaste."* Then I floated gently away, carried by the river of an-
esthesia coursing through my veins.

When I awoke from surgery, my first groggy words were
"Is it still there?" I remember Dr. Ward's face hovering somewhere nearby, her voice soft and reassuring. "Yes, we were able
to spare the nipple. You did very well." With that, I smiled,
shut my eyes, and sank back into the dreamland courtesy of
modern medicine.

The other crucial player in this surgery and in my healing
was, of course, my plastic surgeon, Dr. Keith Attkiss. The first
time I met Dr. Attkiss, I joked that I needed Dr. Ward to save
my life, and I needed him to keep me from killing myself! The

* I am indebted to Dr. John Diamond for his brilliant work on the significance of the nipple as the
highest manifestation of God.

fact that he laughed, that he got the joke, made me trust him from the start. I liked his intelligent face, his calm demeanor, and the clear way in which he explained all the options to me. I tried to ignore the fact that he is extremely handsome and a few years younger than myself, that he had been at Harvard College when I was at Harvard Divinity School, and that I had probably passed him countless times in the Yard without knowing it. Who'd have thought that I would be sitting in his office some twenty years later flashing my poor, battered boobs?

In the end, I was grateful that the two lumpectomies had not done the trick, that I had needed a mastectomy (the very thing I had most feared), because, without it, I could not have had any reconstruction. I would have been left with a mutilated left breast, one that bore no resemblance to what I had had, or to anything remotely attractive. Ironically, because of the dreaded mastectomy, my breast was restored, reconstructed, and healed. Every day, I am grateful to Dr. Attkiss for helping to transform the alien in the mirror, and making it possible for me to find equilibrium and acceptance, a new sense of femininity and power.

For some, there will be no "after." And from these people and their families, I beg pardon for my vanity and my self-indulgent struggles. I am surviving and I am living and I am grateful. Those who have lost loved ones to illness would expect nothing less of those of us who survive. Gratitude. Gratitude and awareness of the chance we've been given to live.

The "after" that I have been given has also deepened my empathy for those who are suffering or dying. I have now tasted the fear of death; I know firsthand what it means to put on that hospital gown, what it does to one's sense of power, identity, and faith. I thought I had understood this before, but now the river runs deeper. As I was going through treatment, the faces of patients I have known, at whose bedsides I have sat, would frequently come to me. *"Did I do you justice?"* I would whisper. *"Were you comforted?"* Clearly, we cannot go back, we can only go forward. Like the scar on my breast, the grooves that have been carved in my heart by my experiences make up part of the intricate mosaic of my life. The more that I embrace what *is,* the more smoothly the pieces fit together; the more I accept myself, the more accepting a presence I will be able to offer to others, in my work and in my life.

About five months after my final surgery, I met a woman whose daughter had died of breast cancer at the age of twenty-eight. Shannon was fitting me for a new pair of cowboy boots when we struck up a conversation. I had noticed the picture of a beautiful young woman hanging from a chain around her neck and knew without asking that this must be her daughter—a daughter who had died. Somehow I also intuited that she was going to tell me the girl had died of breast cancer. So, after a few minutes of trying on boots, I motioned to her necklace, asking softly, "Is that your daughter?"

"Oh yes, that's my girl," she answered, her hand automatically reaching to caress the face on the necklace. "She's my angel now." She straightened her shoulders as if unconsciously preparing to bear the burden again, as if readying herself for whatever her daughter might need, with just the faintest hint of mist in her eyes.

"I'm so sorry," I said. "Is it hard when people ask you about the picture?"

"Oh no," she replied earnestly. "I love when people ask me about her. It used to be hard to talk about it, but now I want to. It's getting a little easier with each passing year. When people ask me about my girl, I feel her close to me." Then she told me the story of her daughter's eleven-month battle with breast cancer, how she had lost her hair—not once but twice—how mad she was, how frightened at times, and how she, as a mother, had come to know that she would lose her girl.

After a while, I shared my story as we stood there in this Western shop in Phoenix. I had just dropped my own teenage daughter off at a ranch camp about an hour north. The woman listened with genuine interest. Then she laughed, confiding that she usually found it hard to be around "you survivors." Why not her daughter? Why wasn't she among the legions of daughters and mothers and sisters and friends who walk for the cure, wear the pink ribbons, and embrace at annual fund-raising events?

I could not (and cannot) answer this. All any of us can do is to listen to each other without judgment. I listened as Shannon told the story of her daughter's struggle, of the anger and the despair, of the chasms it caused in the family, and of the ripples still felt, some three years later. I smiled as she described her daughter's sense of humor, how she could make an innuendo out of anything, how she loved animals and her little brother. I looked again at the chain that bore the picture of Shannon's daughter, smiling there and looking nothing like someone who would die of cancer not long after it was taken.

And I thought of my own daughter, away from me for the first time at a camp in the middle of the Arizona desert. I thought of having to get on a plane and head back to New York, leaving Cat in the care of others. I thought of the unbearable sorrow of every mother who has lost a child. Fear began to creep up my throat as I imagined all of the dangerous possibilities that awaited my daughter—in the desert, in the future, in life—and I was forced to wrestle again with the specter of life's cosmic unpredictability.

To calm myself, I tried to feel what Cat and I had always called the "golden cord." When she was little and wanted to know what her belly button was, I had told her that that was where we had been connected when she was in my belly, that before she could eat or breathe with her mouth, that's where she got everything she needed. "I want to be connected again," she had said earnestly, with her wide aqua eyes. "But you are, sweetheart," I told her. "There is a golden cord that still runs from your belly button to mine. It may be invisible to others, but you and I know it is there. No matter where you are, you will always be connected to me." Whenever she was afraid to do something without me, she would touch her belly button and whisper, "The golden cord, Mommy."

As Shannon and I spoke, she continued to caress the token of her own golden cord. She listened, even though I was one of those "survivors." We giggled as I showed her my boobs and talked about the surgeries. She smiled genuinely, knowingly, and said they looked good. She cocked her head to one side as she contemplated my hair, trying to imagine it long and straight as I had described, rather than short and curly; then she said how cute her daughter had looked bald, and how she had come to wear her baldness with fierce and defiant bravery. She also shared the pain her daughter had felt as she contemplated her own disfigured body. "Who's going to want me now, Mom?" she had cried in anguish. To which Shannon had replied, "Everybody, darlin'. Everybody's gonna want you."

In the end, we stood together—sisters, mothers, friends—exchanging our stories like sacred stones, different, the same, full of mystery and pain. She fitted me with a great pair of cowboy boots and told me to go "kick some ass." Then we embraced, knowing we would see each other again—and her daughter, too—if not in this life, After.

29

ANGELS AND GHOSTS

CONTRARY TO EVERY INTELLECTUAL impulse, I admit that I believe in some sort of afterlife, some on-goingness of spirit. It probably bears little resemblance to what we have been taught or have conceived. This doesn't bother me. Because, truth be told, I believe in the whole kit and caboodle: the transcendence of the spirit, the reunion of souls, guidance from spiritual masters, communion with the dead, and the possibility of reincarnation. That is my confession. In short, I believe in Mystery.

Working as a hospice chaplain for so many years has only fortified this impulse, this irrational, intuitive sense that we are not alone on our sojourns here, and that the life we know is not the end of the road. Some call this faith; others may consider it a foolhardy refusal to embrace our finitude. No matter. The spiritual world is not dependent on our belief, nor is it hindered by our hubris. It simply is.

Through hospice, I have encountered people from many religious backgrounds. All have helped to expand my own ideas and beliefs, and some have allowed me to experience firsthand that which cannot be explained. Growing up Protestant offered a pretty clear-cut spiritual path. There was God, of course, and Jesus (second in command); there were angels God could send to watch over you at night, and there were ghosts who appeared (at least in my house) seemingly on their own, like independent agents. *Ghosts,* of course, is an embarrassing word for spiritual presences. Educated people don't like to admit even the vaguest belief in them, and religious people aren't sure whether they are allowed to. The saints, on the other hand, were something my Catholic friends knew about—they were kosher (to borrow a phrase) spirits but were out of bounds for me. God, Jesus, angels, ghosts, saints . . . all of these point to a reality we cannot see. All indicate the possibility that there is more to life than meets the eye. And when you are dying, it's like realizing you have a parachute—or you can fly.

One of the most comforting thoughts for many people who are dying, and for their families, is that death is a crossing over, that our loved ones are waiting for us, and that we will recognize one another on the other side. It is not uncommon for people to "see" a departed loved one in the days or hours before they die. Hospice professionals know this to be a sign that death is imminent. One might think that this phenomenon is but the result of wishful thinking, medicated delirium, or some sort of brain-wave functioning. Perhaps I would believe this, too, had I not witnessed it time and again myself.

For example, how to explain the case of a fifty-eight-year-old woman with ALS, commonly known as Lou Gehrig's disease. This debilitating disease affects the muscles and the nervous system with relentless and terrifying force. It can begin with the extremities, with the weakening of the muscles in the legs and arms, working its way up to the lungs and throat and face; or it can sometimes present most strongly from the top down, beginning with the inability to swallow or talk, followed by difficulty walking and moving. Because it attacks only motor neurons, the mind is not impaired, nor are the senses. This means that the patient is quite aware of what is happening to his or her body, even while the ability to communicate becomes increasingly inhibited.

This woman, whom I'll call Joan, first experienced a weakening in the muscles of her throat, resulting in the loss of her voice and her ability to swallow. She had a feeding tube for nutrition and, in the beginning, could still write notes to communicate her feelings or carry on basic conversation. Eventually, her writing became illegible, and she had to resort to pointing or gesturing to convey her needs. Through it all, she remained remarkably calm and cheerful, welcoming visitors into her home and always expressing love and gratitude for the daughter who cared for her. Her bravery, like that of some others I've known who have suffered from debilitating diseases, was quite astounding.

One afternoon, shortly after her daughter had assisted her into bed, Joan gestured toward the dresser that sat in the far corner of her room; then she pointed to the window near her bed. "What, Mom? What do you want?" asked her daughter sweetly. She was sitting on the bed with her mother, relaxing in the intimacy between them, born of the care she had been giving her, and of the trust that they shared. Joan gestured again toward the corner, her eyes looking intently in the direction of the dresser, and then the window. "Do you want a tissue?" asked her daughter, surveying the items on the dresser top.

Joan shook her head no.

"Do you want me to open the window?"

Again a slow shake of the head.

"Is it the Chap Stick? Do you want me to put some Chap Stick on your lips? Are your lips dry?"

Still she indicated no.

"Hmmm. I'm sorry, Mom. I'm not sure what you want."

Joan looked at her daughter and smiled, as if to say, "That's okay, honey. I understand. It's hard." Then, with slow, deliberate movements, like one patiently demonstrating a lesson to a child, she pointed once again to the dresser, then to the window. The daughter placed her cheek near Joan's, trying to align herself with her mother's perspective, trying to see what she saw, *how* she saw, from her position on the pillows. Then something caught her eye, and it began to dawn. The picture. The picture of her grandparents, her mother's parents, smiling from within the frame on the dresser.

"Mom, do you see Grandma and Grandpa?"

Joan shut her eyes and nodded, grateful to this daughter who always seemed to get it when no one else could, who persevered in deciphering the gestures and grunts, the nods and eye movements. *Yes.* She nodded. *Yes.* Then she moved her leaden arm toward the window once again, the languid gesture at odds with the fire in her eyes.

"Do you see Grandma and Grandpa at the window?" whispered the daughter, her own eyes sharpening into focus.

A nod. *Yes.*

"What are they saying?"

Joan shut her eyes, summoned her strength, and focused all her effort on her right hand. *Come,* was the gesture. *Come.*

"Well, Mom," began the daughter with a catch in her throat. "If Grandma and Grandpa are here, if they are telling you to come, then it's okay with me. You just go. You just get out of that body and go."

Mother and daughter lay side by side, holding hands in the cozy bed as the sun began to set. A ceiling fan whirled softly overhead, providing more air for those struggling lungs. Four hours later, Joan was gone.

The medical people were surprised. They could not explain exactly why Joan had gone so quickly. By every indication, she should have had several more months to live. But her daughter knew. And as she told me the story, bringing me into the bedroom and reenacting the scene, I knew, too. I gently picked up the picture on the dresser and stood for a moment in the quiet, looking into the smiling faces of Joan's parents. *"Thank you,"* I breathed. *"Thank you for the strength of love it took to come to Joan, to make her see you. Thank you for all the others who will be helped by your story. Take care of Joan, and your granddaughter, too."*

Were they angels or ghosts? I don't know, and it doesn't

matter. We know so little and we understand less. When my own daughter was very small, she was obsessed with angels. Well, angels, fairies, mermaids, et cetera. The world is magical and alive when you are two years old—and anything is possible. And so, when Cat would talk about angels (she was a strangely articulate child), I chalked this up to the wide-eyed wonder and imagination that permeated her existence.

One evening, as I was bathing her, she told me again how much she loved angels. It was early December, and there were angels everywhere—on Christmas cards, in store windows, on top of our tree. I was days away from giving birth to her little brother, adding to the excitement and anticipation. "Have you ever seen an angel?" I asked her casually as she played in the tub.

"Only once," she replied seriously, tilting her chin up to meet my gaze.

"When was that?"

"When they brought me to your tummy."

I figured that someone must have given her this idea, that she must have asked where babies came from, especially given the fact that my belly was increasingly becoming the elephant in the room. Still, she hadn't heard this from me, so I was intrigued.

"Did they say anything to you?"

"Yes," she said with authority. "They said blub-blub-blub-blub-blub."

Actually, she didn't say "Blub-blub-blub-blub-blub," but she said something in a language that I could not understand.

"What did they say?" I pressed.

"They said blub-blub-blub-blub-blub."

The same sounds came out of her mouth. It was strange, because Cat had incredible enunciation for a child her age. She spoke with no baby speech impediments, no cute lisps. And what it sounded like was some ancient tongue.

"I'm sorry, honey, I still don't understand what you're saying."

She sighed, looking at me as if I was impossibly dear but hopeless. Then she said slowly and clearly, to make sure I'd understand, "They said the angels love you, and then they left me there with you."

"How many were there?"

"Two, I think."

"Do you remember what it was like in my belly?"

"Well . . . only that it was sort of pink . . . and I was swimming."

Obviously, Cat had no knowledge of amniotic fluid. She had never seen pictures of babies floating in their mothers' wombs, and she certainly had never been exposed to ancient languages. Afterward, she couldn't repeat for me the words that she had said that night—and a few years later, when I asked her if she remembered being in my belly, she said, "No." Perhaps, fresh from the other side, she could still remember, still hear. Fresh from the world of angels, she could still speak their tongue.

The dying may not be fresh from heaven, but they are nearing it, moving toward it. Maybe they can begin to hear the faint voices of those who've gone on before them. Maybe the muffled sounds of this other life are able to seep through the cracks and crevices of our conscious minds when we turn our attention that way. Perhaps light can be seen under the door through which we all must cross. The dying are moving closer to that door. And just as angels may have escorted us here, perhaps they escort us home.

I would like to think that this was the case for Tina, a forty-year-old woman suffering from devastating multiple sclerosis. A former professional dancer, she eventually became paralyzed and blind, existing in a world of darkness and relegated to the confines of her bed. Tina struggled with the idea of God, of faith, of afterlife. She contemplated suicide but had no means by which to accomplish it herself. She asked me if I would be willing to assist her, saying that she had a friend who could put together the "cocktail." I told her I could never do that, but I could visit her, talk with her, listen to her, and that she wouldn't be alone.

I desperately searched for ways in which to offer comfort and guidance during our visits. We had turned forty together in the months that Tina was on the hospice program—and yet I was living my life filled with family and work and all the everyday pleasures that we simply take for granted. "Tell me about your life," she would say with an eager smile. "Tell me what your son said again and about growing up in Ohio. Bring the world in to me." And so we would share—my life, hers. I would sit beside her bed looking into eyes that could no longer see but could still occasionally dance.

Unfortunately, with each passing week, her suffering became more profound. Her physical symptoms were being well managed, but her spiritual and emotional distress was increasing. She was beginning to feel like she couldn't take it anymore. She just wanted to die, die, die.

One day when I arrived, Tina told me that she had had a strange experience, and that it had scared her a little. She said that she had awoken in the night to find several figures around her bed dressed in ceremonial Japanese gowns. (Her heritage was a mixture of Japanese and Chinese.) "I know I can't see, Andie, but I *saw*. Do you know what I mean? I *saw* these figures around my bed, and it scared me."

"Why do you think they were there?" I asked.

"I think they wanted me to come with them, but I didn't know anyone and I was afraid. When I got scared, they disappeared. Now I wish I would have just gone with them. Why didn't I just *go*?" she moaned.

Tina's mother was still alive, and her father had never been a part of her life. So, unlike others, she had no familiar presence coming for her. And this frightened her. We talked about what the traditional dress might mean. She came to conclude that it was a gesture of respect and celebration. Then we explored the possibility that these spirits might be ancestors, people connected to her in ways she didn't yet know, couldn't yet understand. Perhaps they knew *her* even if she didn't know them. This idea seemed to comfort her.

"Do you think they'll come back for me?" she whispered, tears flowing in silent rivers from eyes that yearned to see again.

"Why don't you ask them, Tina? Invite them. Tell them you're ready."

A week later, she finally let go. While the hospice team was earnestly grappling with the ethical questions of terminal sedation, nutrition and hydration, and how to relieve her existential suffering, Tina bowed quietly and departed.

I would like to know if she saw them again, the elders, the wise ones, the spirits, ghosts, angels, but that is her secret.

Even in the midst of great suffering, it can be difficult to let go. It is a leap into the unknown. For some, this is terrifying; for others it is like going home. Clearly not everyone feels the same way. One's own bed can be heaven. It's like a little girl I knew whose older brother had told her that when she died she would turn into a scary skeleton monster, her skin would all fall off, and she would roam the earth forever. Distraught, she went running to her mother for an answer. "What does happen when we die, Mommy?" she asked.

"Well," her mother began, trying to choose her words carefully. "If you're good, you go to heaven." Although she knew it was simplistic, she hoped that this would satisfy her daughter's curiosity and concern. No luck. Instead, the little girl thought about this for a moment. Then, with a serious face, she replied, "I guess that sounds okay . . . but if I'm really, *really* good, can I just stay home?"

Sometimes the idea of heaven seems nothing like home. Sometimes angels can feel like ghosts, here to startle and frighten us—and sometimes the ghosts are of our own making, those things we carry around from our past to haunt and to torture us. Perhaps that is why we need at times to be angels to one another. We need to get used to the idea of it, the feel of it, the experience of having someone appear in ways that are unexpected and healing. We need to practice being angels ourselves so that we might recognize the real thing when it comes.

During the worst of my treatment for cancer, I had such an angel. His name was Devon, and he was a big, burly guy who ran a parasailing outfit out of Key West, Florida. I was there on vacation with my family, between treatments, between surgeries, and somewhere between normalcy and despair. My kids had wanted to go parasailing, something not remotely tempting to me, and that's how we met Devon.

Out on the blue waters off the coast, we buzzed around. I watched my children dangle sixty feet in the air, my heart in my throat, waving like a lunatic to show them that I was okay with it. *There is my life,* I thought. *There is my flesh and blood and every reason why I want to live.* After a few spins around, Devon noticed the scarf on my head and, I'm sure, the lack of hair along my temples and neck.

"You a survivor?" he asked, in his big, warm voice.

"I'm trying to be." I smiled. "I'm in the middle of my treatment. I've had two surgeries, two months of chemo, and have two more of each to go!"

"Right on!" he said with gusto. "My cousin's a survivor, so I know you must be *strong.* You've *got* to be strong. You're the matriarch, the momma. Right on!"

I felt a whoosh of gratitude wash over me. I'd been a little self-conscious going out on the boat with my scarf under my baseball hat.

"Thanks, Devon, I needed that. Sometimes I feel so strange going out in public like this."

"Why? You should be proud. You're surviving. You're fighting."

Looking into the sky where my children were suspended, pulled by this boat under the charge of this man, I relaxed. *They are in good hands,* I thought. *They are flying, and they are in good hands.*

The next day, I was wading waist-deep in the pool with my son, tossing a ball. Before getting out, I decided to test my "Scuba-do-rag," a sort of funky bathing cap, and go underwater. When I came up, I did so without the cap—it was just me and my bald head in the middle of swimmers and sunbathers. I quickly grabbed the cap and slapped it on my head, inside out. Then I jogged over behind a little cabana. I felt mortified and exposed. As I sat on the lounge chair trying to collect myself, a shadow crossed my path. Devon.

"Hey there, Momma! How ya doin'?"

"Terrible. Did you just see me and my bald head coming out of the water? I'm so embarrassed."

"Come on now, remember, you should be proud. You're strong. You got nothing to be embarrassed about, right, kids? Aren't you proud of your momma?"

I looked up at him in wonder. "You always seem to appear at just the right time! You must be my angel."

"God puts us where we need to be," he said with a smile.

When we were getting ready to leave for New York, I looked for Devon, wanting to say good-bye. I found him and told him again how much his words of encouragement meant to me. Then I took two silver bracelets from my wrist and wrapped them around his. "These are to remember me by. And when I miss them, I will think of you." He enfolded me in a big bear hug and told me he would be praying for me. I started to leave, then I turned around and asked, "By the way, what is the name of your parasailing company, in case we come back?"

"Here, take a brochure with you," he said. When he handed it to me, I just shook my head and laughed. Across a rainbow parasail, against a clear blue sky, were written the words "Almost Heaven."

I guess that's good enough for me.

30

ALLIE-ALLIE-IN-COME-FREE

I am in God's presence night and day—
And he never turns his face away.
—WILLIAM BLAKE

IN THE DARKNESS, A child lies motionless, still as a corpse, barely breathing. All senses are heightened, every cell is alive, each beat of the heart pulsates beneath the surface of gossamer skin, the delicate rib cage rising and falling imperceptibly. The night air is alive and fragrant. It smells of earth and leaves, of moss and wood, and occasionally of some unseen kitchen's roast. The chirping of crickets is almost deafening. Sound is the only guardian; it is the one protection against being discovered. A voice in the distance, a rustle of leaves nearby map the battleground. And just when it seems like the heart can tolerate no more, when the silence has pressed itself too tightly against those ribs, comes the merciful ring of "Allie-allie-in-come-free! Allie-allie-in-come-free!" Rescue at last! Safety at last! The child springs like Lazarus from the tomb, from the purgatory of hiding, to run home, home, blessed home. Into the light, out of the darkness, free from the danger that lurks in the shadows, free from the terror of hiding alone.

I never liked hide-and-seek as a child, especially the way we played it in my neighborhood in Ohio. We called it Kick the Can. On warm summer nights, we would gather, choose the place for the can, choose home base, and set the boundaries for hiding. Someone would be It, everyone else would hide, and the game would begin. If you were found, you became a prisoner until someone was brave enough to storm the base and kick the can, setting you free. Then the quiet would be shattered by tin tumbling across concrete and by the happy shrieks of those who were released once more into the arms of the night.

The can was usually set up near our back porch because of the central location of our house. It sat at the base of a hill with a field to one side and woods to the other. Our playing area was fairly large, encompassing the several surrounding houses, which were separated by hills and trees and creeks. Most of the kids in the neighborhood found it very exciting; I, on the other hand, was terrified.

I never liked being It, never liked setting off into the night alone, heart pounding, wondering if someone was going to jump out and startle me. But I liked hiding even less. Although I enjoyed the thrill of feeling alive and independent, loved the balmy air, loved the way voices would carry, and the challenge of finding a good place to hide, I dreaded the waiting. I was terrified of the waiting, of the anticipation of being discovered, and, even worse, of the idea of being forgotten out there in the dark. If I was never found, would I win the game, or would I be lost forever?

I was good at hiding. I could stay still as a stone as the seeker passed dangerously near. Sometimes, when the silence and the darkness settled in too close around me, I would give myself away, preferring to be caught rather than be imprisoned by the night any longer. And if I did manage to remain hidden, I would strain my ears for the first sign of that blessed bellow: "Allie-allie-in-come-free!" Then I would run down the hill to my house, run toward the warm light of our little porch, and the familiar sound of my parents' voices drifting through the open windows. *I am found! I am found!* I would think. *I survived and I am home.* The porch light would keep the dark woods and the fields at bay while the surrounding houses glowed again like watchful sentries rather than menacing jack-o'-lanterns.

There have been many moments in my life when I have felt as if I were setting out into the darkness alone, setting out in search of whoever might be hiding, whoever might be waiting to be found, to be released from their isolation. This search has led me to the homeless who hide in plain sight before us; it has led me to the bedsides of the dying who wait for release; and it has brought me knee-deep in human remains. When you offer to be It for another human being, you commit yourself to the search, to the dogged task of finding and retrieving the lost, regardless of the possibility that they might not want to be found. You take the chance that, even if you guide someone to the safety of the porch light, he may choose to run headlong back into the woods, back into the darkness. That is not your concern. Your concern is only to keep searching, to keep calling, to keep the light within sight, and to listen.

The times I have hidden in my life are by far the more terrifying. Hiding, we cut ourselves off from the company of others; we decide that it is every person for himself or herself, that the odds are better if we go it alone, and that we will take our chances when it comes to being lost indefinitely. When we hide from ourselves or others, the light which used to signal home seems inaccessible; the voices once recognized as those of friends seem foreign or threatening.

Sometimes this happens with illness. When we, or someone we love, are diagnosed with an illness, especially a serious illness, we often feel like hiding. We don't want to talk about it. We don't want friends to ask us about it; and as we run, the world itself transforms into something dark and unrecognizable. Sometimes we strain our ears to hear if God is coming after us, coming to save us; and sometimes, we are terrified that the only response we will get is the sound of our own blood pumping in our ears.

Remember Kisagotami's search for the mustard seed. Her despair sent her into the darkness of grief, the singular isolation of a heart's refusal to accept what had come to pass. She was hiding from the finality of her loss, and she did not want to be found if this meant being forced to accept her son's death. Instead of lecturing her or even consoling her, the Buddha heard her story and sent her out into the world as a seeker.

Unknowingly, she became It for those upon whose doors she knocked. She sought what any household would surely have, and any person could afford to give—heartache and compassion. After a while, she kept knocking, kept seeking, not because she continued to think it was possible to retrieve the mustard seed, not because life would be restored to her baby, but because life was being restored to *her*. What had died in her was being rekindled—the will to live, the courage to accept, the ability to love. Therefore, instead of returning to the Buddha with a tiny mustard seed, she brought him back a heart of wisdom. And wisdom, as the Buddha knew well, would lead to compassion, and compassion to virtue.

How do we keep God alive in ourselves? How do we bear the things that happen, the things we cannot prevent? We keep moving, keep seeking; we come out of hiding, we listen for guidance, we open our eyes to the light ahead. We talk and we listen, and we sometimes do things that don't seem to make sense to others. The Norwegian novelist Johan Bojer describes something like this in his story "The Great Hunger." He writes:

> An anti-social newcomer moved into the village and put a fence around his property with a sign saying, "Keep Out." He also put a vicious dog in the fence to keep anyone from climbing it. One day, the neighbor's little girl reached inside the fence to pet the dog and the dog grabbed her by the arm and savagely bit and killed her.
>
> The townspeople were enraged and refused to speak to the recluse. They wouldn't sell him groceries at the store. When it came time for planting, they

wouldn't sell him seed. The man became destitute and didn't know what to do. One day, he saw another man sowing seed on his field. He ran out and discovered it was the father of the little girl.

"Why are you doing this?" he asked.

The father replied, "I am doing this to keep God alive in me."

To KEEP GOD alive inside of us when hardship comes is a difficult task. At first, we may die a little inside. Sometimes the inner flame is nearly doused. But this need not be the end of our story. The man whose daughter was killed didn't pretend to forgive the recluse for his daughter's death; he didn't rush right over with a fruit basket or feign some noble acceptance of God's will. No. He watched the townspeople reject this man. He stood by as they forced him into near starvation by not selling him groceries or even seed. The father didn't protest this treatment. On the contrary, his silence spoke volumes about his approval.

Then something happened to him; something happened within him. He realized that each day he spent embittered, each day he lived with hatred seeping into the cracks of his shattered heart, each day he refused to do what he would normally do, namely to show compassion to another person, he died a little more inside. He could not bring his daughter back to life, but he could begin to live again himself. And he did this by the simple act of sowing seed on the field of one who was in need, even though this one was the source of his anguish. With each handful of seed tossed, the flame began to burn again inside of him.

With each row of planting completed, he moved toward something that resembled his life among the living.

God, hope, joy, ultimate meaning, inner happiness, whatever you might call it dies a little in us each day that we choose to hide, choose to cut ourselves off, choose to stop caring about the rest of humanity. And we die. Events like 9/11, like the suicide bombings in the Middle East, like children dying of starvation, like people freezing on the streets of the most affluent cities in the world, these events press into us. They force the heart into hiding because the fear of pain is so great. We become overwhelmed, numb, and our sense of self-protection is ignited. We do not want to see or feel or hear. But if we are willing to open our eyes, we will find God seeking us; if we open our ears, we will hear God calling us—and we can follow that Voice, which beacons us toward the light, toward the best of who we are.

Again I am reminded of Dr. Viktor Frankl, the Austrian psychiatrist and Holocaust survivor. He witnessed murder and experienced cruelty beyond comprehension. He was stripped of his dignity, deprived of his humanity, starved and beaten, yet was still somehow able to experience meaning, still able to feel something like blessing. While working in a trench and feeling that death might be imminent, he described the following:

The dawn was grey around us; grey was the sky above; grey the snow in the pale light of dawn; grey the rags in which my fellow prisoners were clad, and grey their faces. I was again conversing silently with my wife, or perhaps I was struggling to find the *reason* for my sufferings, my slow dying. In a last violent protest against the hopelessness of imminent death, I sensed my spirit piercing through the enveloping gloom. I felt it transcend that hopeless, meaningless world, and from somewhere I heard a victorious "Yes" in answer to my question of the existence of an ultimate purpose. At that moment, a light was lit in a distant farmhouse, which stood on the horizon as if painted there, in the midst of the miserable grey of a dawning morning in Bavaria. *"Et lux in tenebris lucet"*—and the light shineth in the darkness.*

WE ARE HERE to be lights in the darkness. We are here to seek others and to be found ourselves. Keep asking. Keep knocking. Keep calling in the night. Keep listening. God is present.

* Viktor Frankl, *Man's Search for Meaning* pp. 51–52.

ACKNOWLEDGMENTS

I can think of no better way to close this book than with the expression of my deepest gratitude for all of those souls—seen and unseen—who have helped to make it possible.

I am indebted to my agent, Cynthia Manson, whose expertise, intelligence, dogged determination, and faith in me provided the momentum and courage necessary to complete this project. I will always be astounded about how we met—in a church after September 11—and how her ears heard something in my voice that seemed worthy of notice. Without her, this book simply would not have come to be. And I am forever grateful.

It was through Cynthia that I found my brilliant editor, Peter Borland. Like a literary architect, Peter's vision for the book gave it structure and form. He intuited the thread that connects these stories, aligning them with the flow of the Spirit. His insights inspired me to be a better writer, and his friendship encouraged implicit trust in the process. I would like to thank Peter, Judith Curr, Susan M.S. Brown, Tom Cherwin, Adrian James, Dominick Montalto, James Thiel, Davina Mock-Maniscalco, Isolde Sauer, Yona Deshommes, and everyone at Atria for giving me this opportunity.

The beautiful painting which graces the cover is the incredible work of Peter Brooke. Not only is he a gifted artist but he is also, I am proud to say, a friend from our college days at Denison University. How his painting came to be on my cover is just one of the many mysterious things that happened with this book. I am eternally grateful to Peter for his generosity in allowing me the use of "Welling Light." The honor is truly mine.

The canvas upon which I was painted began with my parents, Richard and Lillian Ruehrwein. There are really no words to describe the love and gratitude I have for them. Because the Spirit was alive in them, the reality of God's presence was intrinsically bound to my experience of the world. Faith was a seed deeply planted in my DNA and nurtured by their example. My father's gift for storytelling, his beautiful writing, his creativity, and his voice are the humming foundation for my own writing; my mother's love and steadfast faith provide the lilting tune. Thanks, Mom and Dad, I love you!

For my sisters and brothers—Ray, Jim, Laurie, Jennie, and Joey—who shared my childhood, who continue to be my friends in the world, and who cared for me when I was sick, THANK YOU! Who else would believe the wonderful, funny, strange, and mysterious things that happened in our home? I'm sorry if my brothers were inadvertently slighted in these stories. But, for Joey, whose care and support during my illness inspired him to drive a few hundred miles to build a sweat lodge with his friend, Kenneth Coosewoon—yours is a gift I will never forget. For Jimmy's bravery during the Vietnam War, and for his love, and for Ray's wit, strength, and courage until the day he died, thank you. To Jennie and Laurie: you are not only my sisters, you are my friends. I can't imagine walking this life without you. Thank you for the comfort of your presence, and for the way you make me laugh from the belly of my spirit.

Thanks also to Mac and Sally Gibbons and to Bill and Kate Raynor for over twenty years of love and support.

I am blessed with many friends who make my life richer because of their presence—Brooke, Jackie, Robin, Jenny D., Chris, Tess, Andrea (who probably doesn't realize how much I love her because I'm such a rotten friend!), my Buzz Party girls—if I attempt to name you all, I'm sure to miss someone. Please forgive me. You know who you are and what you mean to me. Thanks also to Bobby for taking my author photo—your professional expertise and your eye for light helped illuminate me.

I must especially acknowledge my soul sister and best friend, my spiritual companion on this journey—Katherine Buechner Arthaud. Her voice is ever a lighthouse in the storm, a safe haven, and a guide. My first editor in the initial drafts of these stories, she is an incredible writer, whose work always humbles me. Perhaps one day she will put her pen to some of our adventures!

To the church of my childhood, Groesbeck United Methodist in Cincinnati, whose people prayed for me while I was ill, and have supported me since my baptism—thank you! Although the theology reflected here might be a stretch for some there, I trust that we are still spiritual kin. And to my current church, Asbury Crestwood in Tuckahoe, New York: thank you for being a congregation of openness and love.

My thanks to the community of Rye, to all who brought dinners when I was sick, and to the Caring Committee who organized them. To Kamal (Ralph) from Playland Market for his kindness, and to Abla for giving me the beautiful scarves, thank you. I will never forget little Hanan trying to teach me how to wear them! Thanks to my buddies, Gerri, Linda, Irmi, and Lisa, at Poppy's for their warmth and humor, to Manfred and Christine at Salzburg Patisserie for their support, to Kelly and the girls at Rags for dressing me and boosting my spirits—and to my beloved Ross and his band of pirates at Piazza for being my "Cheers" family. I would also like to thank the Rye Fire Department for the honor of being their chaplain, and my friend Chief Peter Cotter for bringing me to them.

I have had the privilege of studying with many wonderful teachers: Drs. Walter Eisenbeis and David Woodyard at Denison University, Father Henri Nouwen and Drs. George MacRae and Harvey Cox at Harvard, to name but a few. Some of these great spirits are now gone, but their teachings remain. I would be remiss if I didn't also mention my second grade teacher, Gladys McDine, who told me when I was seven that one day I would write a book (and who made me promise to mention her when I did!). Thanks Mrs. McDine!

I am deeply indebted to Dr. John Diamond, whose brilliant work continues to infuse and inform my understanding of God, of the inherent belovedness of the Soul, and of the healing power of creativity. I have been the humble, and sometimes bumbling, beneficiary of his extensive research, his intuitive genius, and his lifetime of practice. His spiritual insights deepen and expand my own. But I am perhaps most grateful for his wisdom and compassion, and for the many times he has lifted my spirit, gently nudging me back on the path of inspiration and aspiration. Thank you, Dr. Diamond, for being my Teacher and friend.

To the doctors who were instrumental in saving my life—Drs. Barbara Ward, Keith Attkiss, and Beverly Drucker—thank you! Your extraordinary compassion was as important in my healing as your expertise. Thanks also to the nurses and staff of Greenwich Hospital for the excellent care they continue to provide every day; and thanks to my "chemo buddy," Margaret. What would I have done without you!

I will always cherish and be grateful for my years as chaplain of the Jansen Memorial Hospice in Tuckahoe. It was here that I found my professional path and a ministry that continues to challenge and move me. To the colleagues who taught me how to care for the dying, not only with skill, but with tenderness and reverence, to the many families who welcomed me into their homes and hearts, and to the ghosts who still whisper, "Remember how this all began. It began with a family," thank you.

The greatest blessings in my life are my children, Cat and Alex. Everything I do, everywhere I am, is made more meaningful, more beautiful, because they are in the world. I am in awe of their spirits, their gifts, and their courage; and I am grateful for the ways in which they teach me every day. They were my first ears, listening attentively to stories that others would find difficult to hear, offering their wise and loving input over milk and cookies till the wee hours of the night. No essay was ever complete until it received their approval. You two will always be the best part of me—and I will always love you.

To my husband, Andrew—for the long hours sacrificed so that I could write, for the many years you have supported me, loved me, inspired and put up with me, I thank you. Only you could grasp the cosmic glue between us. You will always be the music to the lyrics of my heart.

And, finally, to the spirits of Ground Zero, of hospice, and of heaven: thank you for the privilege of intersecting with you. Thank you for accompanying me on this journey. It is my prayer that you have been honored here.